No Other Help I Know

No Other Help I Know
Sermons on Prayer and Spirituality

Edited by J. Alfred Smith Sr.

Judson Press ® Valley Forge

No Other Help I Know.
Sermons on Prayer and Spirituality
© 1996 Judson Press, Valley Forge, PA 19482-0851

Unless otherwise noted, Bible quotations in this volume are from *The Holy Bible*, King James Version (KJV). Other Bible quotations are from the New Revised Standard Version of the Bible (NRSV), copyright 1989 by the Division of Christian Education of the National Council of the Churches of Christ in the United States of America, and are used by permission. The New King James Version (NKJV), copyright © 1972, 1984 by Thomas Nelson Inc. The New American Standard Bible (NASB), © 1960, 1962, 1963, 1968, 1971, 1972, 1973, 1975, 1977 by The Lockman Foundation. Used by permission. HOLY BIBLE: *New International Version* (NIV), copyright 1973, 1978, 1984. Used by permission of Zondervan Bible Publishers.

Library of Congress Cataloging-in-Publication Data
No other help I know : sermons on prayer and spirituality / edited by J. Alfred Smith Sr.
    p. cm.
  ISBN 0-8170-1251-6 (pbk. : alk. paper)
  1. Prayer—Sermons. 2. Sermons, American—Afro-American authors.
I. Smith, J. Alfred (James Alfred)
  BV210.2.N6 1996
  248.3'2—dc20   96-35562

Printed in the U.S.A.
05 04 03 02 01 00 99 98 97 96
10 9 8 7 6 5 4 3 2 1

To my wife, Joanna Goodwin Smith,
and to Dr. Allan and Mrs. Elna Boesak,
as well as the many anonymous persons
whose prayers have helped to keep me on my feet

Contents

Preface

These sermons on prayer and spirituality come from the head and heart of some of the most celebrated preachers produced by the African American Christian legacy. These preachers speak on the national and international preaching circuit with a frequency that almost equals their Sunday preaching commitments in the churches they serve as pastors or in the classrooms where they serve as teachers of preachers. Their sermons reflect not only excellence in the crafting of sermons according to the methodological principles of textual exegesis and contemporary homiletical construction but also the deep, spiritual ethos of the preachers as persons who maintain daily spiritual intimacy with God. You cannot be in the presence of these preachers long without discovering that they join preacher-prophet Micah in loving mercy, doing justly, and walking humbly with God.

Each preacher represented has known the sufferings, travails, and tribulations that redefine character and define the nature of spirituality. None was born into a family of privilege and prosperity, but each was nurtured by parents who were powerful because they lived in the presence of God. Their souls have been dyed by the practice of prayer, and they are conscious of God's presence permeating their purpose and productivity as God's preacher-prophets. As my friend Dr. James Washington of Union Theological Seminary would say, these preachers are not "morticians of spirituality, but trustees of a living spiritual endowment."[1] God forbid that we take this rich legacy of prayer and spirituality for granted.

Resources for the survival of persons of ebony hue have
not been as available as they have been for persons who trace
their lineage back to the Mayflower. Those who date their
genesis on American soil back to the slave ship of 1619 and
those who survived the ugly middle passage as well as the
demonic passages of slavery and segregation have found
through their sole resource of prayer that they knew no other
help but God. So they as well as their offspring prayed. May
this tradition of piety and prayer continue into the twenty-
first century.

Reading these sermons on prayer and spirituality will
tune readers into the high frequency of communication with
the Eternal, who calls each of us into a communion that offers
a healing and holistic salvation not found in the secular
world of competition, conquest, and control. May these sermons become a vital and viable aid in assisting the readers
to know no other help than that which comes from stretching
our hands upward to God in prayer. Our troubled times
mandate that we remember that we have no other help but
God.

Dr. J. Alfred Smith Sr.

1. James Melvin Washington, *Conversations with God: Two Centuries of
Prayers by African Americans* (New York: HarperCollins, 1994), p. 283.

Acknowledgments

I wish to express most of all my love and gratitude to my wife, Joanna, for her patience, poise, and prayers, which sustain me in my puny efforts as a Christian servant.

My thanks also go to: the contributors, who know that life is fragile and that it must be handled with prayer; co-pastor, J. Alfred Smith Jr., and a loving and cooperative pastoral team, who gave me time to work as a studious editor on this project; the officers and members of Allen Temple, who are always affirming and encouraging; and minister Cheryl Elliott, who is an excellent prayer coordinator.

I also wish to acknowledge Marjie H. Lawson, who without any complaining worked very closely with the editorial staff at Judson Press and the contributors so that all deadlines could be met. She transcribed the sermons and typed many pages over and over in order to assist me in presenting to Judson Press a professionally prepared manuscript.

Inestimable assistance has also come from Mrs. Carlotta Holmes-Herbert, Executive Secretary, for the great help she has given me in handling many of Allen Temple Baptist Church's administrative details, so that my mind could be freed to concentrate on my manuscript. She has carried out these duties in a very cheerful manner.

Last, but not least, I wish to thank the editorial staff of Judson Press, who have the highest of journalistic standards.

xii

Their counsel was immeasurable. I am grateful for their assistance.

Contributors

Charles E. Booth is pastor of Mt. Olivet Baptist Church in Columbus, Ohio. He holds degrees from Howard University (B.A.), Eastern Baptist Theological Seminary (M.Div.), and United Theological Seminary (D.Min.). He also serves as professor of preaching at Trinity Lutheran Seminary in Columbus.

Harold A. Carter is pastor of New Shiloh Baptist Church in Baltimore, Maryland. He has earned doctoral degrees from St. Mary's Ecumenical University and Colgate Rochester/Crozer/Bexley Hall Seminary. A writer and evangelist, he has led crusades across the United States.

Suzan D. Johnson Cook serves as pastor of an American Baptist new church development project, the Bronx Christian Fellowship, Bronx, New York. She holds an M.A. degree from Teachers College, Columbia University; an M.Div. degree from Union Theological Seminary; and a doctorate from United Theological Seminary. She is the editor of *Sister to Sister: Devotions for and from African American Women* (Judson Press).

Kevin W. Cosby is pastor of St. Stephen Baptist Church in Louisville, Kentucky. He earned an M.Div. degree from Southern Baptist Theological Seminary and a D.Min. degree from United Theological Seminary.

Frederick D. Haynes III is pastor of Friendship-West Baptist Church in Dallas, Texas. A popular speaker at conferences and schools, he is active in community affairs. He is a graduate of Bishop College and Southwestern Baptist Theological Seminary.

Ella Pearson Mitchell has preached and taught across America for over five decades. She earned an M.A. degree from Union Theological Seminary, New York City, and a doctorate at School of Theology, Claremont, California. She is editor of four books of sermons by African American women preachers.

Otis Moss Jr. is pastor of Olivet Institutional Baptist Church in Cleveland, Ohio. He holds a B.A. degree from Morehouse College, an M. Div. degree from Morehouse School of Religion/Interdenominational Theological Center, and a D. Min. degree from United Theological Seminary. He has been widely recognized for his community involvement and religious leadership.

James C. Perkins is pastor of Greater Christ Baptist Church in Detroit, Michigan. A well-known speaker and writer, he founded the Fellowship Nonprofit Housing Corporation, an organization dedicated to community economic development, and the Benjamin E. Mays Male Academy. He is a D.Min. graduate of United Theological Seminary in Dayton, Ohio.

Jini Kilgore Ross is co-pastor with her husband of New Vision Baptist Church in Katy, Texas. She is also instructor of English at Houston Community College in addition to her work as writer and editor. She has edited two books of sermons by Jeremiah A. Wright Jr. and is a contributor to several books of sermons. She earned her M.Div. degree from the American Baptist Seminary of the West in Berkeley, California, and a Master of Arts in journalism from the University of California, Berkeley, California.

Gary V. Simpson is senior pastor at The Concord Baptist Church of Christ in Brooklyn, New York. He holds degrees from Denison University (B.A.), Union Theological Seminary (M.Div.), and United Theological Seminary (D.Min.). He has preached throughout the United States and lectured at Drew, Union, New Brunswick, and New York theological seminaries.

Jeremiah A. Wright Jr. is pastor of Trinity United Church of Christ in Chicago. He is a graduate of Howard University (B.A., M.A.), the University of Chicago Divinity School (M.A.), and United Theological Seminary (D. Min.). His writings include *"What Makes You So Strong?"*: *Sermons of Joy and Strength* and *Good News! Sermons of Hope for Today's Families*, both from Judson Press, as well as *Africans Who Shaped Our Faith* and *When Black Men Stand Up for God*.

1

The Blessings of Unanswered Prayer

2 Corinthians 12:2-9

Charles E. Booth

Prayer is the cornerstone of the Christian pilgrimage. Prayer is petition, supplication, requisition, entreaty, appeal, call, beseeching, imploring. In the Christian context prayer can never be seen as a monologue—one-way communication. Prayer is a dialogical experience because it involves the petition of the mortal and the response of God. Someone has said, "Prayer is a long-distance telephone call from the heart of man to the throne-room of God." Someone else has said, "Prayer is the sweet perfume of the rose of Sharon that lifts us with its heavenly fragrance." Our mothers and fathers placed the significance of prayer in these lines: "Jesus is on the main line, tell him what you want, tell him what you want right now. Call him up, call him up, tell him what you want right now!"

Most of us feel that if we enjoy a good relationship with God, we can expect the Almighty to answer our prayers in the affirmative. Seldom, if ever, does one pray anticipating a negative response. The Bible is replete with instances in which God grants prayer requests. Consider the following:

1. The children of Israel prayed that God would get them out of bondage, and finally, after four hundred years, God did.

2. Jochebed prayed for the baby of her loins, and her prayer was answered when Pharaoh's daughter lifted the child from her bathing pool and named him Moses.

3. The children of Israel prayed for sustenance and received manna, quail, and water in answer to their requests.

4. Jacob prayed that Esau might finally receive him in peace, and he did.

5. Hannah prayed for a son, and God gave her Samuel.

6. Daniel prayed for deliverance from the lions' den as did the Hebrew boys from the fiery furnace, and both requests were heard.

7. Solomon prayed for and received wisdom to rule the people of God.

8. Jesus prayed over the loaves and fish, and five thousand were fed.

9. Jesus prayed for Peter that he might not be sifted like wheat, and Peter became a power in the church.

Our forebears read these stories and prayed that we might be the recipients of a brighter day, and, bless God, that prayer has been answered.

Let us now flip the coin and look at the other side. There are times despite the closeness of our relationship with God when he chooses not to answer our prayer requests. At worst we are angered, and at best we are disappointed. Abraham prayed that God would spare Sodom and Gomorrah. God did not. David prayed that the child of his illicit relationship with Bathsheba would be spared. The child died. Jesus prayed that he might bypass the cup, and God said no!

Douglas MacArthur, the most decorated general of World War II and the one who promised the people of the Philippines he would return, desired to be president, and God, in his providence, said no!

One would think that someone as close to Christ and as filled with the Holy Spirit as was Paul would have had his every request answered by God. Paul spoke in tongues, had the gifts of discernment, prophecy, healing, and teaching. There was poetry in his voice and fluidity in his pen; yet there was something for which he prayed three times, and the Lord thundered back no! The twelfth chapter of 2 Corinthians begins with the apostle Paul trying to relate an experience he had while being caught up in the spirit of Christ. He says he was caught up in the "third heaven," paradise. He was, in the language of Bishop James A. Forbes Sr., "out of this world." Paul saw things too powerful to utter. Yet, when we come to verse 7, Paul is yanked out of his ecstasy and is made to eat the bitter fruit of reality. Paul says, "And lest I should be exalted above measure through the abundance of the revelations, there was given to me a thorn in the flesh, the messenger of Satan to buffet me, lest I should be exalted above measure."

Paul spoke of a "thorn" in his flesh. In Greek, the word is not "thorn" but "stake." There was a driving "stake" in Paul's flesh that caused him great havoc and pain. What was this thorn, or stake, in Paul's flesh? Many interpretations have been offered throughout the ages:

   1. John Calvin said it was a spiritual temptation. There was something that made Paul want to doubt God and shy away from his apostolic responsibilities.
   2. Martin Luther said it was the pain of always having to face opposition and persecution.
   3. Roman Catholics said Paul's thorn was carnal temptation, since Paul was not married and practiced celibacy. Roman Catholics testified that when monks

and hermits locked themselves up in cells and monasteries, the last natural instinct to be tamed was sexual desire.

4. Perhaps Paul suffered from epilepsy, a painful and recurrent disorder, prevalent in the Mediterranean world, that produced visions and tremors. This interpretation is difficult to accept, because if we claim that Paul suffered from epilepsy, then we would have to question the many visions that he speaks of throughout his epistles.

5. Tertullian and Jerome suggested severe headaches.

6. There are those who suggest that Paul suffered from eye trouble. After his conversion on the Damascus road, Paul was temporarily blinded. Could it be that Paul suffered from some residual eyesight problem? We recall that Paul did write to the Galatians, "See what large letters I make when I am writing in my own hand!" (6:11).

7. Some believe that Paul suffered from virulent malarial fever, which caused one to burn up with fever and produced a grinding, boring sensation in the temples. This disease was common to those living on the coasts of the eastern Mediterranean world.

Most scholars lean toward virulent malarial fever as Paul's "stake" or "thorn" in the flesh. Whatever the stake, whatever the thorn, the bottom line is this—God chose not to answer Paul's prayer request. Paul could not name it and claim it. Paul was not guilty of some deeply entrenched sin. The denial of Paul's prayer request leads me to believe that there must be a blessing in unanswered prayer because God is not cruel, unjust, or sadistic. God derives no pleasure in making or seeing his children suffer. What then are the blessings of unanswered prayer as 2 Corinthians 12 reveals them?

Recognizing Who Is in Control

The first blessing of unanswered prayer comes in the recognition that I am not in control of my life and destiny. I am not, in the language of William Henley, "the master of my fate" and "the captain of my soul." The text in 2 Corinthians 12·7 says that Paul's thorn is "the messenger of Satan to buffet" him. Even though Satan is responsible for the thorn in Paul's flesh, we must realize that Satan could not inflict the thorn except for the permissive will of God. It was not God's absolute will that Paul suffer with his infirmity, but the fact that God allowed Satan to inflict Paul speaks of God's power in permission. This suggests to me that God knows what is best for us. Thank God that *God* is in control.

Can you imagine what life would be like if we had carte blanche in the determination of our destiny? What would happen if we were really in the driver's seat of our lives? What if God were not ultimately in control of our lives? What if God allowed the founding fathers of our republic to really enforce Section 1 of Article 2 of the Constitution, the one stipulating that African Americans are only three-fifths of a human being? What if the Dred Scott decision of 1857 were left unchallenged? What if *Plessey v. Ferguson* of 1896 were left to stand? What if George Wallace's cry at the University of Alabama—"Segregation today, segregation tomorrow, and segregation forever"—had been left unchallenged? What if Adolf Hitler's plan to exterminate the Jews had not been stopped? What if God had answered Martin Luther King Jr.'s prayer that he would become the president of a predominantly black college or university? What if God answered the prayers of our enemies? What if God gave us the green grass on the other side of the fence that we so desperately think we want? What if the South African government had been allowed to get away with the death of Steve Biko and the imprisonment of Nelson Mandela? These are thought-provoking questions that shake me from center to circumference. We must take blessed comfort in the fact that *God* knows best what we need.

Exercising Humility

The second blessing of unanswered prayer is this: despite my spiritual accomplishments, I need something that will keep me in a state of humility. Paul says at the beginning and again at the end of 2 Corinthians 12:7, "lest I be exalted above measure." With all of Paul's gifts—tongues, prophecy, teaching, discernment, healing—there was a need for him to remain humble. Let us not forget his background as revealed in Philippians 3:5: "Circumcised the eighth day, of the stock of Israel, of the tribe of Benjamin, an Hebrew of the Hebrews; as touching the law, a Pharisee." It is no wonder God had to knock Paul down on the Damascus road! It was not simply the body of Paul that was being knocked from his beast, but the ego of Paul had to be dealt with also.

There is something in each of us that bends toward arrogance and pride. We are, therefore, in need of a disciplinary tool that will keep us in check. It is for this reason that God sometimes chooses not to remove our thorns, stakes, infirmities, or hardships. It is his desire that we be completely obedient to him and not become intoxicated with our gifts, talents, abilities, and educational attainments. All of us know individuals who have allowed their gifts, achievements, and attainments to intoxicate them. There are individuals who feel that they are spiritually, intellectually, and academically superior to others. We must never allow the ego to reign supreme when it comes to spiritual matters.

I recently heard a preacher define *ego* as "easing God out." There are times when we do ease God out and become very much enamored with those things that he has given to us for service. There are times when God, of necessity, has to drive a thorn into the flesh that we may not be exalted above measure. The next time you are prone to wonder why God has not answered your prayer, think for a moment about an area in which you might need to be tempered. I am reminded of one of the great hymns of the church that speaks to this issue:

> *Have Thine own way, Lord! Have Thine own way!*
> *Thou art the potter, I am the clay!*
> *Mold me and make me after Thy will,*
> *While I am waiting, yielded and still.*

Realizing the Sufficiency of Grace

The final blessing of unanswered prayer comes in the realization that God's grace is all-sufficient. Paul said he besought the Lord three times for the removal of his thorn, but the Lord replied, "My grace is sufficient for thee." Thank God for his unmerited favor! What I want, the grace of God says I may not need. God's grace is sufficient despite my stake or impediment.

All of us recognize that there are moments in our experience when we need to rely totally upon the grace and the goodness of God. There are times when we cannot rely upon our self-sufficiency. It is in these moments that we recognize we are not as independent as we think. We depend upon God because God is able to direct our paths and lead us in the way everlasting.

Thank God for the blessings of unanswered prayer. We can look beyond the apostle Paul to Jesus Christ our Savior. One needs only to recall the night in which our Lord prayed in the garden of Gethsemane. On the night before his crucifixion, Jesus Christ, the Son of God, prayed three times that the cup might pass. Jesus recognized that crucifixion and death were imminent. As Jesus approached the moment for which he had come into the world, he recognized that his death weighed more heavily upon him than he recognized. He, therefore, wanted to escape what he knew to be his destiny. When he considered the cup and all that it entailed, he asked the Father for its removal. Jesus saw bitterness in the cup.

Jesus saw denial in the cup. Jesus saw betrayal in the cup. Jesus even heard himself questioning his Father. With these realities clamoring in his spirit, Jesus beseeched the Father that he might be granted the answer to his prayer and escape Calvary. Jesus asked the Father three times to remove the cup, and God refused to answer this prayer request of his Son.

If God had answered the prayer of Jesus, he never would have gone to Calvary. Without Calvary, there would be no shedding of blood. Without the shedding of blood, there would be no remission of sins. If God had answered this prayer request of Jesus, then Jesus never would have said, "Father, forgive them; for they know not what they do" (Luke 23:34). If God had answered the prayer request of his Son, then Jesus never would have said to the dying thief on Calvary, "To day, shalt thou be with me in paradise" (Luke 23:43). If God had answered the prayer request of his Son, then we never would have heard the words, "It is finished" (John 19:30). If God had granted the prayer request of his Son, we never would have heard the words, "Father, into thy hands I commend my spirit" (Luke 23:46).

If the Father had granted Jesus his prayer request, then Jesus would have never gone to Calvary. And without Calvary, the sting could not have been taken out of death, nor the grave robbed of its victory. Our Christ is a wonderful Savior because he "was in all points tempted like as we are, yet without sin" (Hebrews 4:15). Even Jesus Christ had to discover the all-sufficiency of God's grace. Despite the Father's love for the Son, God could not grant Jesus' request. Christ had to suffer! Christ had to bleed! Christ had to die! Even the Son of God had to become subject to God's resounding no! Had the Father not said no to his Son's prayer request, there would have been no Calvary. And without Calvary, there would have been no resurrection morning.

Sure I must fight if I would reign;
Increase my courage, Lord;

I'll bear the toil, endure the pain,
Supported by Thy word.

(From "Am I a Soldier of the Cross?"; words by Isaac Watts.)

2

The Living Legacy of
Dr. Martin Luther King Jr.

As Seen through the Streams of Prayer
Psalm 1:3

Harold A. Carter

I once heard Dr. King say in a sermon on nonviolence that
the one who prays ought to work as though the answer to
one's prayers depended upon oneself and not totally upon
the power of God. I was a third-year student at Alabama State
Teachers College in Montgomery, Alabama, when I heard
Dr. King proclaim those words. I was always gripped by the
power of his messages. To me, the Word of God came alive
when I heard him preach. No one could tell our story, that is,
the story of the African American faith pilgrimage in this new
world, quite like him. As I listened to him preach the gospel
in the Dexter Avenue Baptist Church in Montgomery, I was
particularly moved by the power of the oral prayer tradition
of black people, which strongly influenced his life's work.

Little did I know then that I too was being shaped by much
of this tradition, which I had gained quite naturally in my
own home and church environment. My father and mother

were leaders in the church. Their preaching, teaching, and
music ministries had afforded me the privilege of growing
up in a Baptist school, where I received a daily dose of the
song and prayer traditions of my elders. I had also followed
my father as he pastored churches in the rural communities
of Alabama and had felt the impact of his spirit and his mind
as a scholar in Old and New Testament thought. My mother
had been gifted with a great singing voice and was always
serving in leadership capacities in local church and associa-
tional activities. Being surrounded by prayer, praise, and
proclamation was a constant influence on my developing
life.

This background was the motivation that opened my
mind and my heart to hear all that Dr. King had to say about
the goal for liberation and emancipation so deeply longed
for in the African American communities of the 1950s and
1960s. Segregation was then the legal law of the land. A brief
retrospective look quickly informs us that the nation's educational system was mostly closed to black people. An economic ceiling in the social, civic, and business worlds kept
black people locked in poverty. Add to this the fact that black
people were denied the right to vote, which meant that
political representation could not become a reality. The
"white church" itself had opted to help enforce these social
divisions rather than seek the path of liberation and salvation
for all the people. Conditions were grim indeed when Dr.
Martin Luther King Jr., a twenty-eight-year-old preacher of
the gospel, came on the scene, striving to redress the evils of
an institution of slavery and Jim Crowism that seemed almost impossible to change.

What was it that made Dr. King's life so powerful, so
prophetic? What was it that made him the living "tree
planted by the rivers of water"? What unique vision did he
possess that made him the prophetic storyteller of a people's
pain and struggle in a way that convinced them they could

indeed overcome? It is vitally important that we find the answers to these questions.

I want to identify some streams that nourished the life of Dr. Martin Luther King Jr. and made the ministry of prayers so powerful and so redemptive in his life. I am absolutely convinced that these powerful streams are yet available if only we turn to them and drink from their living waters for salvation and liberation in our own times.

Good Soil

The first stream I point to is the soil. Psalm 1:3 says that the good life, the holy life, must be planted: "And he shall be like a tree planted by the rivers of water, that bringeth forth his fruit in his season; his leaf also shall not wither; and whatsoever he doeth shall prosper." Implicit to this idea of planting is good, rich soil.

An essential component in the revelation of all the world's major religions, soil demonstrates that only God is sovereign, for we all need God for seed, rain, and harvest. We all need God to overcome life's known and unknown problems.

Out of the interdependence that the soil produced, family structures were born, families were nurtured, and elders were respected. Humanity learned the meaning of prayer, the way of worship, and the pitfalls of the secular. If there were no soil, there would be no earth . . . no soil, no place to be somebody . . . no soil, no sustenance, no life.

May God forbid that we grow so far in our false understanding of the power of our age as to assume we no longer need the intervention and the salvation of God. Our present-day high technological culture is a marvel to behold, but we must be careful not to make it the idol of a lost generation. We still need one another. We still need God. In the words of Psalm 46:10-11, we are called to "be still, and know that I am God: I will be exalted among the heathen, I will be exalted in the earth. The LORD of hosts is with us; the God of Jacob is our refuge."

Suffering

The next stream that made prayer so potent in the life of Dr. Martin Luther King Jr. and the civil rights movement is suffering. Through several hundred years of slavery and lynchings, black people had been forced to suffer. Then a prophet of God came on the scene and declared that suffering is redemptive when it is done to further the cause of freedom and emancipation! Suffering is redemptive when it is done to exalt faith and to declare one's own dignity as a dedicated servant of God! To fail, not to suffer, not to stand up and even die if necessary for the cause of truth and justice, is to be less than a man, less than a woman! This was the gospel fire that inflamed the hearts of those who heard and followed the steps of Dr. Martin Luther King Jr.

Today we must ask the question, What are we collectively suffering for? What causes have we as a people identified today for which we are willing to suffer and even die? Oh yes, people are dying today, but they are dying for the wrong reasons. They are dying for things that do not save and for worldly vices that do not heal. Drug wars are killing many. Loss of hope and the power to dream have cut many lives short of development. Instead of being trees planted by the rivers of living water, too many are drowning in the brackish streams of passion and poison. Somehow, someway, we must rediscover our deeper selves and collectively rise to the occasion. We must realize that the only suffering that makes sense is the suffering that builds lives, nurtures families, and lifts up standards of equality and opportunity for all of God's people.

There is a government in Washington today that is cutting back so many essential programs the poor and desperate of our nation have depended upon. Shall we sit still and do nothing? Shall we as a church go on living as though people are expendable? God forbid that we do this! We must find new strength in suffering with those who suffer. We simply cannot afford to be warm when the homeless are cold. We cannot afford to be full when men and women and children are hungry. We must spend our lives in suffering for the redemption of others.

Song

Another of those living streams that made prophetic prayer so real in the life of Dr. Martin Luther King Jr. and so potent for the civil rights movement is song. Songs did not start with this movement, for African Americans had sung their way through slavery. Their innate spirit, so attuned to the biological and cultural history of their past, forced upon them the reality of song.

Our African American forebears sang to communicate with God. They sang to feed their spirit. They sang to keep balance in an unbalanced world. They sang, "Steal away to Jesus! Steal away, steal away home, I ain't got long to stay here!" They sang, "Go down, Moses, tell ole Pharaoh, Let my people go!" They sang, "We are climbing Jacob's ladder!" They sang, "Ezekiel saw the wheel, way up in the middle of the air!" They sang, "Were you there when they crucified my Lord? O! Sometimes it causes me to tremble." They sang, "Oh what a beautiful city . . . twelve gates to de city, hallelu!" They sang songs that flowed out of their hearts.

The stream of music made our African American forebears a people with an indomitable spirit. No people who have a song can be destroyed. Take away a people's song, and you take away their very heart. Today we still need the joy of celebration that a song can give. We can pass along our history through song. We can pass along our triumphs and our tragedies through song. We can join hands and hearts with those who have gone before us, and with those who may indeed follow us, through song. This was the bright light of the civil rights movement. It is also a light we need to see shining in our world today.

At the height of his ministry when Jesus was about to go to Calvary from an upper room, we read that Jesus and the

disciples sang a hymn. Why did Jesus do so? He sang because
Gethsemane was ahead, because Calvary was a reality, and
because he was declaring for all eternity to know that Satan
was a liar. His truth, his ministry, would forever march on!

We must be careful that we do not permit the impersonal
and cold, callous atmosphere of today's world to keep us
from singing our song. We still need the radiant theme of our
ancestors singing anew in our lives. "We shall overcome! We
shall overcome!" Deep in our hearts, we will keep on working and believing that "we shall overcome someday"!

Sorrow

There is another stream that provides strength in the hour
of prayer—the stream of sorrow. What is sorrow? Sorrow is
that living chord that ties my life to the pain in another
person's heart! Sorrow is that pain that comes upon us not of
our choosing.

Sometimes sorrow is the burden we bear by virtue of the
color of our skin. It is knowing you are right with God while
the world declares you are wrong. Yet out of the field of
sorrow, you are nurtured. You are refined. You are molded
and shaped until you come forth as pure gold. We are indeed
in good company when we look at the true power of sorrow,
for Jesus Christ our blessed Lord was "a man of sorrows, and
acquainted with grief" (Isaiah 53:3). It was through his sorrow, his ultimate sacrifice of giving his life on a cross, that we
can now have atonement with God.

We must rediscover through prayers of faith and dedica-
tion to service the meaning and redemptive power of sorrow.
Faith comes alive when we serve God through sorrow! Faith
comes alive when we bring life to the hopeless by identifying
with their need. Oh, that our leaders in Washington and
across our nation would discover and rediscover the power
of prayer that comes through the revelation of sorrow. When
this is done, we will see a new spirit of redemptive service
sweeping over our land.

Service

Earlier I told you that Dr. Martin Luther King Jr. declared that our prayers should find us working and serving God as though the answers to our prayers depended on us and not simply on the action of God. He said this because he knew that God was already on the side of right! God had already revealed to us that he would release the captives and set the prisoners free! God had already shown us that he would open up Red Seas and knock down Jericho walls! God had already shown us that he would feed hungry mouths and raise up the dead! God had already shown us that he would give his Son to die for our redemption and to destroy the powers of death, hell, and the grave. What then were we waiting for? It was up to us to go out and to possess the land! It was up to us to build by faith the beloved community.

Nothing fundamentally has changed in God's provisions for us today. We still need to help one another! We still need to nurture our youth and build strong families. We still need to work to see that our sons and our daughters receive the best education possible. We still need to play less and work more, to complain less about what others are doing to us and to collectively do more for ourselves. Only then will we be those trees of life planted by rivers of water that bringeth forth good fruit in our own season.

These, then, are the nourishing streams that can nurture in us a life of powerful prayer. As Martin Luther King's prophetic prayers grew out of these rich experiences, so ours will too. Let all of these streams flow into political life, educational life, community life, everywhere you go, and you will have a prayerful shout.

We are a people of a "shout"! The fact is life needs a shout that happens in sacred places. Why must all our shouts be in the sports arena? Why must all our shouts be in casino halls? Why must all our shouts be in Super Bowls and worldly arenas? The greatest shout is the shout of the soul! The greatest shout comes from bearing fruit in your own season.

Many have laughed at our shout! Many have said our shouts
came out of ignorance! Others declared our shouts came out
of uninformed emotions! Some claimed our shouts came out
of cheap religion. But those who have said these things were
in fact revealing their own ignorance, their own brackish
waters of death.

The Lord our God told us these words, "Blessed are ye,
when men shall revile you, and persecute you, and shall say
all manner of evil against you falsely, for my sake" (Matthew
5:11). When they do this to you, shout! Rejoice! Do not
become bitter! Do not give up! Do not declare that God is
dead! When they do this to you, they are afraid of your
power! When they do this to you, they stand in fear of your
God! When they do this to you, they know that power
beyond human control is working on your side.

Oh, sisters and brothers, do not permit the evil forces of
today's world to seal up your flow of joy. Let your prayers
be shouts of glory in honor of God! Shout glory because our
battle is not won in a Super Bowl. Our battle was won on an
old rugged cross! Our triumph was sealed in our Lord's
triumph over death! Our shout is grounded in the truth that
our God never fails.

Like Moses, we may never see on this earth all the sights
of the Promised Land! Like David, we may never see all our
dreams fulfilled! Like Paul, we may never see all the people
of the world turning to Jesus Christ as Savior and Lord. But
those who are the redeemed of the Lord will be a part of the
ultimate, final shout! Yes, we will overcome because the Lord
our God is on our side. This is our faith! This is our struggle.
This is our living and eternal prayer: Surely goodness and
mercy will follow us all the days of our life, and we will dwell
in the house of our God forever! Amen and amen!

3

Where Are Your Roots?

Ephesians 3:14-21
Suzan D. Johnson Cook

As an African American people, we have always known the importance of affirming who we are. Slavery and the toll it has taken hurt deeply because of the rejection of our contributions and our very humanity. I was not introduced to our history in my own formal education. Only with the persistence and insistence of my family and friends who were educators in the New York City public school system did I learn early in my life to develop an Afrocentric view of myself.

My grandmother was diligent about affirming me and telling me to go to school and share who I was with my classmates. And then in the seventies, the late Alex Haley introduced the now famous television miniseries entitled *Roots.* This series forged a new positive direction for me and many of my peers, for we felt that the truth, however painful it might be, was at least being told and that we were finally being included in the American story. Thereafter, the next generations of wide-ranging ethnicities began to demand equal representation, time, and status. So, for much of my early adult life, much of what I heard was focused on being centered in our culture and heritage. And certainly we all want positive images for ourselves and the generations who will follow.

But for us, as Christians, to focus on our heritage alone is not enough. We must always look to Jesus, the author and finisher of our faith, if we are to be a people who not only look forward but who also go forward. Paul, the author of today's text, calls the people of God together, with all their cultural and societal differences, and reminds them that all are important to God. In Ephesians 3:17-19, Paul says,

> That Christ may dwell in your hearts by faith; that ye, being rooted and grounded in love, May be able to comprehend with all saints what is the breadth, and length, and depth, and height; And to know the love of Christ, which passeth knowledge, that ye might be filled with all the fulness of God.

That is, when we get together under God's umbrella, we are Christians, and they will know we are Christians *not* by our color but by our love and our rootedness in Christ. And so today I ask you, Where are your roots? Alex Haley wrote about his, but do you *live* yours? Where are your roots today?

Paul's letter to the church at Ephesus is a moving and powerful book. In fact, in the last chapter Paul bolsters his readers with the words: "Be strong in the Lord," that is, have power. But we cannot get to the end and speak about power until we go to the beginning and speak about our roots. Paul indicates very clearly that this is a prayer for the people of God—that they be rooted, not in just anything, but in the love of Christ.

Our text is contained in a passage in which Paul describes himself as bowing down on his knees for the people to the Father, of whom the whole family in heaven and on earth is named. So, in order to know where our roots are, we have to know who our father is. God, a very present help in time of trouble, is our parent and unites the family as one. Every sabbath morning is really a family reunion. Yes, we are getting together with our family. That's why Scripture teaches us in Hebrews 10:25 not to forsake "the assembling of ourselves together," because the family needs one another. Oh yes, we do. You may not want to need one another, but you do.

What Paul is calling us to, in prayer, is the strengthening of the inner person. People in the world speak about strength and power in a worldly sense. In other words, people in the world recognize who has the most "juice" or influence or who can lift the heaviest weight. But these are false kinds of strength. Real strength is when you are able to stand, even when your legs are not working, to speak even if you have no voice. Because strength in the Lord is on the inside, no one can see it. But we know when it is there because it is strength in spirit. Paul does not want us to be strong just for the sake of being strong, but to be strong so that Christ may dwell in our hearts by faith. And with that faith comes rootedness and groundedness in love. Where should your roots be? In love.

As a kid, I used to spend my summers in the South; it was one of the favorite and most memorable times of my life. One of my observations back then was that the roots of a tree determined how that tree would stand. The roots were not on the surface; I could not see them. But the longevity of the oak tree told me the roots were there. The abundant fruit on the apple tree told me the roots were there. The blossoms on the magnolia told me the roots were there. Another observation from those summers is that you have to dig *deep* for the roots. Because the roots all stick together, it isn't easy to get them out of the ground. And the longer a tree lives, the deeper the roots. And you know what else about roots? They have soil all in between them. The deeper the roots, the more soil there is.

These images of trees, roots, and soil can teach us much

about our prayer life and study. The more we pray and the more we study God's Word, the deeper our roots should be. As Christians, our soil, that which holds us together, is the Holy Spirit. Deep roots and immeasurable soil help us withstand the world's battering winds. Rooted people should stick together, in Christ. With deep roots of faith and the Holy Spirit, we can be like trees "planted by the rivers of water" (Psalm 1:3) and we "shall not be moved" (Psalm 10:6).

I know about my roots, and I am proud of my roots. As an African American woman, I come from good stock. I came from a legacy of women and men who were not moved, who stood their ground, who spoke out against that which was evil, who marched and did not get weary, who soared to the stars. My roots include women like Mae Jemison, the first African American woman to become an astronaut; Barbara Jordan, who stood proud in Congress; and my own mother, Dorothy, the first woman in New York State to head a security firm, who made sure I felt good to be a young black woman.

And even though I stand on the shoulders of great men and women, I must have my own roots. I must have roots that dig deep into the Christian soil so that when my body wearies and the winds of adversity blow, I shall still stand. My rootedness begins, as Paul began in our text from Ephesians, with prayer, not just for myself but also for my people. My rootedness must be in Christ. And my rootedness takes love, unconditional love, supernatural love, powerful love so that I, too, may be filled with the fullness of God.

I want everything that God wants for me. That's what Jesus wanted. And so Jesus prayed at every crossroad and at every mountain and at every valley. You will find Jesus when you pray. Jesus was rooted in God, who received him back after Jesus did what he was supposed to do for us. And Jesus loved—loved unconditionally—for that is the essence of God. God so loved us that he gave us Jesus, that whosoever believeth in him should not perish, should not lose his or her rootedness, but shall have everlasting life. Amen.

4

Prayer Can Be a Real Eye-Opener!

2 Kings 6:17-23
Kevin W. Cosby

The gift of sight is one of the greatest gifts we humans possess. To look through those little windows we call eyes and behold the beauty, grandeur, and majesty of all that is God's creation is one of life's greatest experiences. Of the five senses, sight is the most essential for the gathering of data and information about our world. Indeed, we learn through observation.

When the Bible speaks of sight, however, it is never something limited to mere retina activity. We know from God's Word that it is possible to have 20/20 vision and still not be truly sighted. Conversely, it is possible to be legally blind and yet be fully sighted.

The former pastor of the famed Madison Avenue United Methodist Church in New York City, Dr. Ralph Sockman made a profound observation to a former generation. Dr. Sockman said that humans have the capacity for three levels of sight. First, there is physical sight, or retina activity. This

level of sight can be evaluated by an optometrist through the
use of an eye chart. Second, there is mental sight. For example, your accountant seeks to unravel the intricacies and
complexities of some new tax law. Finally after much discus-
sion, you begin to comprehend what the accountant is presenting, and you say, "Oh, I see." This form of sight is
different from retina activity because it deals with intellectual
comprehension as opposed to physical observation. Third,
there is what Sockman calls spiritual sight. This form of sight
is the ability to see the providence of God in the midst of life's
trials, traumas, tribulations, and turbulence. A person with
spiritual sight can weather a series of bad breaks with radiant
optimism because through the eyes of faith that person has
seen God working.

Those prophets, priests, artists, seers, and visionaries who
have aided in the moral and spiritual development of our
world possessed spiritual sight. And our slave foreparents
possessed this form of sight in great quantity. Engulfed in a
world of slavery and oppression and stripped of their culture
and human dignity, our slave foreparents held on to a faith
that saw God's presence in the midst of their pain. Songs like
"I got a robe, you got a robe, All God's chillun got a robe"
reflected the slaves' ability to see beyond auction blocks,
cotton fields, and their subhuman status, to see their own
self-worth and God's providential care.

Of the three forms of sight—physical, mental, and spiritual—the latter is the quintessential form. It is the quest for
spiritual sight that is the focus of our text, which is found in
2 Kings 6:17-23. The king of Syria had been waging war
against Israel, but he had been unsuccessful because at every
turn Israel was able to anticipate his every move. All of his
carefully thought out battle plans were met with utter defeat.
Whenever the king of Syria tried to ensnare the king of Israel
in a trap, the king of Israel was always able to avoid it. This
happened with such regularity that the king of Syria became
suspicious, drawing the conclusion that a traitor within his

ranks was supplying the enemy with battle plans and strate-
gies.

In a summit meeting with his generals, the king of Syria
shared his suspicions and asked, "What man do I have who
is for the king of Israel? Who is the traitor in our midst?" One
of his officers answered, "O king, your diagnosis is incorrect.
It's not some man in your army who is making trouble for
you. Instead, there is a man on the other side with whom God
communicates. Therefore, all of the secrets whispered in the
privacy of your bedchamber are told to this one man." The
king asked, "Where is this one man? If one man is the
hindrance, then this one man shall be removed." So thereafter, the king of Syria gathered a great army about him and
sent them forth under the cover of night to seize the lone
prophet Elisha, who was residing in Dothan.

What a tribute the king of Syria unconsciously paid to this
lone prophet of God. Imagine sending a great army,
equipped with all the accoutrements of war, to startle, terrify,
and capture the plain, simple prophet of God. Institutions of
oppression are always threatened by those to whom God has
given spiritual insight. Therefore, prophets should not be
alarmed when they are the victims of harassment, smear
campaigns, tactics of terror, and intimidation. Jesus had his
Caiaphas; Paul had his Nero; Dietrich Bonhoeffer had his
Hitler; and Martin Luther King Jr. had his J. Edgar Hoover.
And each of these persecutors join the king of Syria and other
oppressors throughout the centuries in sharing the same
folly, that is, in believing that through implements of war,
papal encyclicals, decrees from counsels, government legis-
lation, incarceration, physical torture, and death, they can
thwart God's will. The United Negro Collge Fund has used
a line from Maya Angelou's poetry that captures the full
essence of oppressors' folly: "You may write me down in
history with your bitter twisted lies, you may trod me in the
very dirt but still like dust, I'll rise."

The king of Syria along with his men arrived at Dothan at

night. The city was on a hill surrounded by a wide plain. With the men and the horses and the chariots surrounding the city, there was, humanly speaking, absolutely no possibility of escape. The next morning, when the servant of the prophet arose and went outside, he was seized with fear. All around him he saw ranks upon ranks of Syrian soldiers. Based on what he saw with his physical eyes, he concluded that there was absolutely no chance of escape. He and his master were doomed to be captured.

To him, the servant hurried back to tell the prophet that all was lost, that everything was hopeless, and that capture was imminent. When Elisha heard of the predicament, he fell on his knees and began to pray. We should not be surprised that the prophet prayed. Whenever a person is beset with problems and burdens and deliverance seems impossible, it is a normal response to pray. No, we are not surprised that the prophet prayed, but we *are* surprised by the content of his prayer. He did not pray "Sweet hour of prayer," "I need Thee every hour," "Come by here, Lord, come by here," or "Father, I stretch my hands to Thee; No other help I know." Instead the prophet prayed, "Lord, open his eyes that he might see."

Elisha's prayer was a prayer of intercession for his servant. Though the prayer suggests that the servant was blind, his blindness was not physical. The servant could see the horses, the soldiers, and their instruments of destruction; however, this was the limit of his sight. He was devoid of spiritual sight, which left him blind to the presence of another army. If all we see is the physical, we are not truly equipped for life, because the physical represents only a small fraction of what really exists.

The marvel of science is not that scientists invent anything, but rather that they see and discover what always existed but for some reason was unseen. Leonardo da Vinci saw flight in the fifteenth and sixteenth centuries, a few hundred years before the Wright brothers took off from Kitty Hawk.

Thomas Edison did not invent electricity; he simply saw what was always there. George Washington Carver did not place medicine in the peanut but, through spiritual sight, saw what was already there.

It is essential that the artist also be able to see the unseen. A story about Michelangelo describes him as approaching a crude, unfinished piece of marble and saying, "Give me my hammer and chisel as I release the angel imprisoned in the marble." Stevie Wonder was once asked if there was anything worse than being blind, and he said, "Yes, having eyes and not being able to see." Though most of us are able to see, our sight is one dimensional. We only see the seen. We cannot see the unseen. We only see problems and miss the solutions. We only see the burdens and miss the blessings. We only see the fault of our friends and miss their strengths. We only see the victimization and not the victory. We only see racism and not resilience and resolve to overcome. We only see the armies that are against us and not the God who is with us.

Some of us, in fact, are guilty of inventing troubles that do not exist. This form of paranoia is expressed in such remarks as "everybody's talking about me," "nobody likes me," and "no one understands me." Many of us have a trouble factory in our house. When troubles do not come naturally, we go to our trouble factory and create artificial ones. For example, an old lady once came to our church distressed. Her neighbors were running a crack house right next to where she lived. She proceeded to tell me that her neighbors would not leave her alone and she had no one to help her. I stated that lawyers in our church could be of assistance, but she said, "I can't afford one." I invited her to church, and she said, "I have no ride." I told her our church van would pick her up, and she said, "I don't have any good clothes." I told her she could come as she was, and she said, "I would not feel comfortable in pants." All she could see was the problem; she could not see the solution. Does she remind you of anyone you know?

Think for a moment about this piece of advice: If you want to get an assessment of a piece of property, don't ask a buzzard to do the survey. The buzzard will look down upon the landscape, where there are carpets of green grass and where flowers spill out winsome fragrances, but the buzzard will never see the flowers. Instead, the buzzard will zero in on a decayed piece of flesh hidden away in the weeds, because that is all the buzzard has the capacity to see.

Jesus said that the pure in heart would *see* God, but sometimes we lose the capacity to see because of sin. You know, there are a lot of Christian buzzards. They don't see their opportunities for growth, usefulness, and joy; instead, they focus on the negative and dwell on the disastrous. There are female buzzards who gather together at buzzard shops, commonly known as beauty shops, saying there are no good men. One buzzard starts talking with other buzzards joining in to reinforce each other's buzzardness. There are male buzzards who only see racism, oppression, and victimization.

Yes, racism and oppression are real. Yes, the scapegoating of the black male and the criminalization of his image are real, but that is not all there is to see. Ask Booker T. Washington. He saw racism, but that is not all he saw. He saw Tuskegee. Ask Madame C. J. Walker. She saw racism, but that's not all she saw. Before James Brown said it in the 1960s, she saw that black is beautiful. Ask Mary McLeod Bethune. She saw illiteracy, but she also saw discarded chairs and desks that could be transformed into instruments of learning and enlightenment. Ask Ben Carson. He saw Siamese twins being disconnected and living fruitful, independent lives. Ask Berry Gordy. He saw many closed doors, but that is not all he saw. He saw America dancing to Marvin Gaye, The Temptations, The Four Tops, and The Supremes.

How is this kind of sight developed? The text in 2 Kings 6 says that Elisha prayed that his servant's eyes might be opened. Prayer is a real eye-opener. But many of us doubt the efficacy of prayer because we think of it as a magic lamp we rub to make genies come out and do our bidding. When the genies don't come, we begin to doubt the utility of prayer. However, the real value of prayer is that it enlarges our sympathies, quiets our mind, sweetens our disposition, widens our perspective, soothes our spirit, purifies our thoughts, and calms our anxieties. Indeed, prayer opens our eyes.

When the servant's eyes were opened, he saw that encompassed about the Syrian army was the army of the Lord with horses and chariots of fire. God was always there, but the servant had not been aware of it. God is not an absentee God, for God is always here. God comes in unexpected ways and at unexpected times, but God is always present. God comes through the tired feet of a Rosa Parks. God comes through the imprisonment of a Nelson Mandela. God comes through the uprising of a Nat Turner. God comes through the nationalism of a Malcolm X. God comes through the political activism of a Jesse Jackson. Paul Tillich says that God is present in the spirit that makes us restless with injustice and evil in the world.

Prayer is a real eye-opener because it opens our eyes to the reality of God's presence in all of life's circumstances. Living life with an awareness of God's presence and providential care enables us to overcome the Syrian threats in our lives. When we see God, it is impossible to see hopelessness, despair, gloom, and defeat. When we see God, enemies become less significant. When we see God, we see a way in the midst of steep mountains and low valleys. When we see God, we have victory in the midst of ill-wishers, backbiters, hole diggers, joy stealers, dream busters, and depression makers. It is not that these people don't exist, but we know that God is greater than any who are against us.

God's grace is greater than our sins; God's presence is greater than our fears; God's healing is greater than our sickness; and God's resurrection is greater than our death. Psalm 27:1-3 declares:

> The LORD is my light and my salvation; whom shall I fear? the LORD is the strength of my life; of whom shall I be afraid? When the wicked, even mine enemies and my foes, came upon me to eat up my flesh, they stumbled and fell. Though an host should encamp against me, my heart shall not fear: though war should rise against me, in this will I be confident.

5

Prayerfully Handling Situations beyond Your Control

Acts 12:1-16

Frederick D. Haynes III

Is there any problematic predicament that leaves you with the feeling that your hands are tied or that your hopes are handcuffed? This haunting helplessness especially plagues persons who care about individuals and institutions snared in situations that they need to get out of, caught in miserable mazes that appear to have no exit, and imprisoned by perplexing problems for which there appear to be no answers or assistance. "I wish there was something I could do" is the compassionate, yet excruciating, cry of those handcuffed by helplessness and anguished in the awareness that there is little or nothing they can do to direct someone or something they care about out of an imprisoning impossibility.

This story has been told of Max Lucado. In the predawn hours of a Sunday morning, Lucado went to his church office with excited expectancy. In order to enter the building, he had to unlock the door and punch in the code to the alarm system. After entering the building, he rushed to the alarm system's

keyboard and punched in the code. Nothing happened. He
tried it again. Nothing. With undiscourageable determination laced with heightening urgency, he tried it again—to no
avail! Time was running out. Suddenly the siren blared,
floodlights inundated the hallway, and red strobes turned.
Lucado kept pushing buttons, and the alarm kept blaring.
He raced down the hallway and called the phone company.
The technician he spoke to inflamed his frustrations. "Yes, I
punched in the code; it didn't do any good," he responded
to an obviously stupid question. Finally, a police officer
showed up. Handcuffed by helplessness, Lucado cried out
to the officer above the loudness of the eardrum-beating
siren, "I can't get the thing to shut off." Calmly, the policeman
inquired, "Are you the preacher here?" "Yes," Lucado
confessed. The officer shook his head and walked away. Soon
thereafter the siren ceased.

When was the last time you attempted to solve a perplexing, yea, painful predicament by pushing buttons that would
not respond? Have you known the frustration and apparent
futility of trying to fix a shattered situation? What about the
aggravation that comes from trying to help someone who
doesn't really want to be helped? Have you been assaulted
by anxiety while hoping for the best but expecting the worst,
with your anxiety amplified by the awareness that there is
nothing you can do to remedy or resolve the situation?

Are your hands tied? This is the predicament of a parent
in pain because a child is the captive of crack cocaine. This
disposition of dismay is felt by one whose loved one is
locked up in a dysfunctional relationship, a prisoner of
physical and emotional abuse. This pessimistic posture is
felt by one who must helplessly watch a loved one who,
as a prisoner of pain incarcerated by an incurable illness,
is playing "hide and go seek" with death. Perhaps you are
in a situation in which your back is against the wall. You feel
imprisoned in an impossible circumstance—your future is
foggy, and the present is precarious. Hopelessly handcuffed,

all you can do is hope for the best, while in your heart of
hearts you expect the worst. Are the odds against you? Do
you feel overwhelmed because what you need far exceeds
what you actually have? Is the challenging crisis that
confronts you also confining you and threatening to conquer
you?

The early church was navigating through treacherously
turbulent times. Their backs were against the wall. Herod
had decided to make political scapegoats of the Christians
in order to increase his standing in the Jewish public-opinion
polls. It is a dark day when politicians and people in power
produce policy that is created by crowd consensus and not
the convictions of conscience. Herod used his position of
power as a tool of oppression instead of as an instrument of
service, empowerment, and liberation. James was executed,
and when Herod discovered that the slaying of James pleased
the Jews, he decided to kill the drum major, the leader of the
unarmed, politically vulnerable, socially ostracized, and
stigmatized Christian church, Simon Peter.

Peter was arrested simply because Herod decreed it.
Peter's rights were disrespected, and justice was denied
simply because of who Peter was and how he had been
labeled. Victims of racism and sexism in what Maya Angelou
aptly describes as "these yet to be United States" readily
identify with the circumstances of the Christian church and
the predicament of Peter. The church was the convenient
scapegoat of a politically insecure king, who had to hold
someone else down in order to build himself up. Manifesta-
tions of this scapegoat syndrome, which occurs when an
unstable economy causes an insecure, visionless leader to
attack the defenseless and the disinherited, are not limited
to ancient times. Present-day devotees of the syndrome attack
and assault affirmative-action programs and other efforts to
empower the disadvantaged and the dispossessed. My
mother, with pointed, picturesque profundity, portrays the

scapegoat syndrome with these words: "They will steal your eyeballs and then blame you because you can't see."

Peter was incarcerated without "due process." Justice had been denied, but Peter and his friends in the faith could do nothing about it. The power of Herod stood against the predicament of Peter. Herod had political power in his hands; Peter was handcuffed. Peter's predicament is replicated over and over again. Herod controls the paycheck that you need in order to survive. Herod finances the drug traffic that holds a community socially and economically hostage. In the corporate world, Herod will give you a position with no power and establish a glass ceiling that limits upward mobility. Furthermore, Herod will set you up in order to take you out. At home, Herod is the authority figure who is physically, psychologically, and emotionally abusive.

Herod had in his hands power that he used and misused in order to abuse, while Peter had his hands tied and appeared to be helpless. Herod was on the throne; James had been executed and buried; Peter was in jail and was scheduled to die early the next morning; and the church was handcuffed by helplessness. However, notice the momentous, yet subtle, shift of momentum in Acts 12:5, the shift occasioned by the words "but prayer." Peter was in prison, "but prayer . . ." Herod was on the throne; James had been executed; Peter was incarcerated, a victim of the scapegoat syndrome; the church was handcuffed by helplessness, "but prayer . . ."

If your uncontrollable situation is going downhill fast and you feel as if all you can do is stand on the sidelines of that situation with your hands tied, insert "but prayer" in the paragraph of your predicament, and the momentum will subtly, yet surely, shift. When your problematic predicament is beyond your control, prayerfully take it out of your hands and put it in the hands of the one who is in control and who can put your situation under control by orchestrating deliverance in, from, and out of any situation.

Prayer of Intercession

How do you insert "but prayer" in the paragraph of your problematic predicament and prayerfully handle a situation that is beyond your control? A perusal of Acts 12 inspires and invites us to a prayer of intercession. When faced with the crisis, the church discovered and demonstrated that when our hands are tied, they are positioned for prayer. The church did not call a business meeting, they called a prayer meeting. They assembled in the home of Mary, Barnabas's aunt, the mother of John Mark, the site of the upper room. This location was loaded with magnificent memories and meaning. This sacred site, which had become the holy headquarters of the soldiers of the Savior, allowed them to assemble in an atmosphere replete with reminders of what God had done for them. Here they could pull out their faith file and be encouraged by redemptive replays of God's awesome activity on their behalf. Here they had received the Lord's Last Supper. Here they had experienced a resurrection appearance of their liberating Lord and victorious Savior. Here they had prayed after the ascension of Jesus. Here they experienced and had been infused with spiritual power on the day of Pentecost. Here they prayed for boldness and had been filled with the Holy Spirit after being threatened by the religious authorities. Here the place had been shaken.

The climate of prayer allows you to pull out your faith file and reflect on and rejoice over what God has already done. Replaying divine highlights from your walk with God in days past will fortify your prayer with faith. Dr. Harry S. Wright, one of my professors at Bishop College, truthfully testified in class, "I know what God can do, based on what he has done." When your hands are tied and you feel helpless, remember prayerfully when God's hands have moved on your behalf, "making a way out of no way," opening and shutting doors, dispensing blessings, defeating enemies, providing direction, and facilitating deliverance. Prayer

creates a climate of reflection on what God has done and
injects us with faith about what God is able to do.

In Acts 4, after Peter and John had been threatened by the
leaders of the religious establishment, the two disciples went
to Mary's house and reported to the company of Christians
what had taken place. They all united in prayer. And in this
prayer, reflection provided petition:

> Indeed Herod and Pontius Pilate met together
> with the Gentiles and the people of Israel in this city
> to conspire against your holy servant Jesus, whom
> you anointed. They did what your power and will
> had decided beforehand should happen. Now, Lord,
> consider their threats and enable your servants to
> speak your word with great boldness (Acts 4:27-29).

They prayerfully reflected on God's awesome track
record and were injected with faith and boldness to face
their present predicament.

When the church gathered for prayer as recorded in Acts
12:5, they interceded on behalf of Peter. Intercession
literally means "to pass between." Intercession allows us
to stand between God and the situation or person for which
we are praying and seek God's intervention on behalf of
that situation or person. One of the faithful deacons in this
church is kind enough to service the cooling unit in my
home. One sweltering summer afternoon, the cooling
system failed to function. Upon rushing to my family's
rescue, the deacon quickly ascertained that the source
of trouble was a nonfunctioning relay switch. Not the
source of power, the relay switch is the channel for the
power, that is, it accesses our home to the power source.
When the relay switch was replaced, the unbearable heat
gave way to a comfortable climate.

Intercession allows us to serve as "spiritual relay
switches," channeling the power of God into situations
sweltering with the heat of stressful impossibilities. Many of

us today are the beneficiaries of spiritual relay switches, a praying grandmother, grandfather, father, mother, teacher, pastor, or loved one who went to God on our behalf when we did not have the sense to pray for ourselves. Many doors have opened, have been prayed ajar, by spiritual relay switches, who accessed heavenly power for our hellish predicament, thereby reordering our wayward steps in a divine direction, providing us with what we needed when we needed it, and rescuing us from something we had gotten into that we desperately needed to get out of.

Note that the church's prayer of intercession as described in Acts 4 was earnest and enduring. The word used in this passage is the same word used to describe the intense prayer of the Master in the garden of Gethsemane. This was no flippant, casual prayer meeting where the believers repeated well-worn prayer phrases. This was no empty exercise or routine religious ritual, but intense spiritual interaction that eventuated in a powerful transaction on behalf of Peter. The actions of these early believers demonstrate that if our prayers are to mean anything to God, they must mean everything to us. My ministerial mentor, Dr. Manuel L. Scott Sr., tells the story of a little boy who was asked, "Do you ever say your prayers?" He, with innocent insight, responded, "Sometimes, I say my prayers, but then there are times when I pray my prayers."

The believers, the spiritual relay switches, interceded intensely on behalf of Peter. They did not just say their prayers, they *prayed* their prayers. Furthermore, they prayed in partnership. They prayed as one people in one place for one purpose. There are some situations so dire and desperate that a "Lone Ranger" approach won't do. Jesus assures us of his presence and power when we have a "quorum" of two or three who agree in his name. It is difficult, if not impossible, for me to pick up an object with one finger. It is improbable, and highly unlikely, that I can pick up many objects with two fingers. However, if I use all five fingers in concert, the hand can pick up anything that is in my strength to lift. As individuals, no matter how strong we may be spiritually, there are some things we cannot handle by ourselves. We need partners in prayer who will join with us in lifting persons, predicaments, incidents, and institutions to the receptive ears of our heavenly Father.

Note that the church prayed for Peter in spite of what had happened to James. James, you remember, had been killed at the hands of this same ruthless Herod. The believers could have easily reasoned that their prayers would not make a difference in the situation of Peter. It is tempting to prematurely and pessimistically conclude that because God did not intervene on one occasion that God will follow the same pattern on another. However, Scripture reminds us that his ways are not our ways (see Isaiah 55:8).

We also must keep on praying in spite of what has happened to the Jameses in our lives. Some disappointing situation that did not work out according to our liking should not preclude us from praying and should not tempt us to give up on God and prayer. We must continue to pray even when things do not work out for James. John Madden, the football commentator, spoke appreciatively of the remarkable running back Emmett Smith. In a game between the Dallas Cowboys and the Oakland Raiders, Smith was having an awesome game. To illustrate the greatness of this illustrious record-setting running back, Madden created a new statistic that he labeled YAC, standing for "yards after contact." Smith gained over fifty yards after an opposing player hit him and attempted to stop him. Herein is Smith's greatness—in his determination to go on in spite of obstacles and opposition. The test of our faith is determined by our spiritual YAC. What do we do after we have been hit by bereavement? Do we keep on after we have been hit by some disappointment? Do we dare to keep on praying after a situation does not turn out the way we hoped it would? How is your spiritual YAC?

Providential Intervention

When we confront a situation beyond our control and are handcuffed by helplessness, we can insert "but prayer" into the paragraph of the predicament, thereby interceding through prayer This will lead to providential intervention. In this regard, someone has sagaciously suggested that prayer moves the hand that moves the world.

The church prayed in Acts 12:5, and God dispatched an angel in verse 7. The timing of God's intervention in response to the prayer of intercession is noteworthy. Our slave foreparents packed a ton of truth into a teaspoon of terms when they triumphantly testified, "He may not come when you want him, but he's right on time." God answers prayer not according to our time but according to God's time. Peter had an appointment arranged by Herod with a guillotine early the next morning. However, God rearranged Peter's itinerary and used an angel to answer the prayer of the supplicating saints.

Peter slept soundly between the guards. He was on death row, in maximum security, sleeping on the eve of his scheduled execution. Perhaps Peter went to sleep comforted by these words of the psalmist: "He that keepeth Israel shall neither slumber nor sleep" (Psalm 121:4). Perhaps Peter reasoned that if God cannot sleep, there was no need for both of them to lie awake. So Peter went to sleep. The angel had to hit Peter hard in order to awaken him.

It is tragic, yet true, that some people for whom we pray have gone to sleep in their situation, are content, and have developed a level of comfort in some imprisoning predicament. It may be unhealthy, but they are comfortable. It may be an abusive relationship, but they are content. It may be an addiction to a substance, a situation, or a person, but they have gone to sleep. Charles Dutton, the brilliant African American actor who went from jail to Yale and starred in the meaningful series *Roc*, was asked why he was not a repeat offender like so many other exconvicts who, upon being released from prison, find that opportunity is limited and fall back into a life of crime. I was told that with dignity Dutton declared, "The difference between me and those who are repeat offenders has to do with the fact that when I was in jail, unlike all of the other prisoners, I refused to decorate my cell." Many people are locked in some negative circumstance and have decorated their cell. They have become comfortable in a bad situation. However, when we pray for them, God is able to use an angel to hit them in hard in order to wake them up.

After the angel awakened Peter, it was necessary for the angel to free him from the chains that bound him in the prison. It may be necessary for God to free some people *in* their predicament before he can free them *from* their predicament. When Shadrach, Meshach, and Abednego were thrown in the furnace of fire, God freed them *in* the furnace before he freed them *from* it. When Nebuchadnezzar looked to ascertain the condition of the young men, he discovered that though they had been thrown in the furnace bound, they were freely walking around with a divine escort. When God answers our prayers for others, he may have to free them *in* the situation before he frees them *from* it.

Peter had been chained to at least two guards from the four squads of soldiers assigned to watch him. The angel severed the chains that shackled Peter to the guards and instructed the apostle to put on his clothes. Peter complied. The angel then led Peter out of the prison, and he was free. You see, Peter's deliverance was not complete without direction.

Peter's divine deliverance took place at night because God works the night shift. When the night is dark, God is not done. When we cannot see our way clear, God works the night shift as our light in dark places.

The Scriptures are sprinkled with illustrations and insights about God's night-shift activities. When Moses and the Israelites got to the Red Sea, they heard the prancing hoofbeats of the horses pulling the chariots driven by Pharaoh's soldiers. The Israelites were caught in a geographical cul-de-sac: imposing, impassable mountains stood on both sides of them, and the sea lay before them. However, God caused an east wind to blow until the waters parted and the wind paved a freeway through the Red Sea. God works the night shift. One midnight, after having been thrown in jail, Paul and Silas were praying to and singing about the God who works the night shift. God ordered an earthquake to shake up the place, and the jailhouse was rocked. Paul and Silas went free, but not before witnessing to a terror-struck jailer about God. God works the night shift in response to prayers of intercession. When this takes place, prepare for the incredible.

Prepare for the Incredible

When Peter came to his senses, he realized that God had providentially intervened and secured his release from prison. He quietly rushed through the streets of the city to the home of Mary, where the anxious saints were interceding on his behalf. He knocked on the door. The servant girl Rhoda inquired, "Who is it?" Peter excitedly made himself known. However, Rhoda was so excited herself that she forgot to unlock the door and rushed back and reported her good news to the assembly of anxious believers fervently praying for Simon Peter. The answer to their prayers was locked outside! When Rhoda informed them that Peter was at the door, they accused her of losing her mind. They were praying for Peter, yet they were not expecting God to come through. Could it be that they were praying with diminished expectations because of what had happened to James? They weren't prepared for the incredible. Often our prayers are empty exercises devoid of expectation because of our poisoned preconceptions. Because of what did or did not happen to some James in our lives, we pray not expecting anything to happen.

The church prayed for Peter, but they weren't ready for him when he showed up as the answer to their prayers. How unfortunate it is that when God answers our prayers and Peter shows up, we don't know what to do with him or how to deal with him. This happens when wayward children, for whom parents have prayed, make a U-turn and attempt to do the right thing, but parents (and churches) allow negativity to dominate their attitude and refuse to let them live down what they used to do. This happens when a husband or wife prays for the spouse to change but allows what *has been* to preclude him or her from expecting or accepting what *can be*.

When you prepare for the incredible, you can be energized by expectancy and therefore tailor your attitude and activities to anticipate what God will do. When this happens, we can experience what the intercessors experienced in verse 16. The text says that they were "astonished." Synonyms for the word *astonished* include *shocked, stunned, flabbergasted,* and *amazed.* However, the word that arrested my attention and depicts their disposition is *surprise*! When you prayerfully intercede, God will providentially intervene. You should be prepared for the incredible when God moves in such a mighty way that you hear him shout through the awesome answer to your prayers, "Surprise!" Has God ever surprised you? Just when you were about to give up, God showed up and shouted, "Surprise!" Good Friday was horrible and dark. Jesus, heaven's hero and earth's emancipator, had been crucified on a cross. He was buried along with the hopes of his followers in a tomb. Early Sunday morning some women went to embalm the body of their dead Lord. However, when they arrived at the tomb, an angel, who had been working the night shift, shouted, "Surprise! He is not here! He is risen!"

When your hands are tied by helplessness, insert "but prayer" in the paragraph of your predicament, for God is able to intervene by orchestrating deliverance and punctuating the paragraph of your predicament with his surprise!

6

Women of Faith

James 1:5-8

Ella Pearson Mitchell

It could be said that women might be more spiritual because we have been brought up to be more influenced by "right brain" functions. That is, women are more at home in the spiritual and emotional, while men are more at home with the facts, figures, and hard data of "left brain" functions. It is believed that women seek the assistance of counselors more than men do. And membership statistics of churches show that there are more women members, which suggests that we also seek God more than men do. However, the question is How, in what frame of mind, do we seek God? Are we strong, accountable, wise? Are we women of faith without doubt? That is the challenge of our text for today.

Our text comes from the setting of early Christians under trial. In James 1:2, James the servant of God advised Christians to count it all joy, even when violent threats face those who keep the faith. In verse 4, James suggested that they should "let patience have her perfect work." And in verse 5, James advised that if they lacked wisdom or if there were any problems understanding their persecution, they should ask God for strength and spiritual wisdom to handle them. God is glad to give such wisdom and does not fuss or scold

people for wanting answers to their questions. Then in verse
6a, James says, "Ask in faith, never doubting." Verse 6b
describes people who doubt as divided in mind, going up
and down like the waves of the sea. In a word, prayer for
wisdom demands an unwavering faith. One can never understand or deal effectively with trials and tribulations—will
never have strength—without unwavering faith.

Within the bounds of this understanding, the certainty of
the promise is, oh, so awesome. This wisdom *will* be given
to any of us. Furthermore, the offer for help stands—there
is no expiration date on it. If we approach God with an
unshakable faith, a tenacious trust, we will have no lack of
wisdom or strength. Our understanding will measure up to
our need, no matter how old or young, no matter how
educated or uneducated, no matter the IQ. And, of course,
our complete trust will help us avoid the very appearance
of trying to call God on the carpet to account for our tribulations.

Let me give an example of what I mean. Many years ago
my husband received a phone call from a very dedicated
layman who had been double tithing and working sacrifi-
cially in the churches of northern California for many years.
This logging contractor had just had his eyes blown out of
their sockets by a charge of dynamite, which had acted as if
it weren't going to go off at all for forty-five minutes. When
he went to check it out, he lost both eyes. This now sightless
saint was asking Henry, "What on earth is God doing? Why
did he let this happen to me?"

My poor husband didn't know what on earth to say, but
he was finally led to offer, "God works for the good of those
who love [God]" (Romans 8:28, NIV). Then he suggested the
friend offer a prayer that went something like this: "Dear
God, I trust you, even though I haven't the slightest idea
what good you can possibly bring out of this. But I know
you will bring something good. I hope you will bear with

my great curiosity. Please, Lord, let me know the answer soon."

As I look back, I wish so much that nearly fifty years ago we had seriously studied James 1, for then we could have been more helpful to our friend. We could have asked him to turn to James 1, inviting him to count it all joy. We could then have suggested a strong biblical base for the advice that he be careful about challenging God as if God were a doubt-ful and suspicious equal!

Years ago, a black sister wrote a hit show on Broadway with the title *Your Arm's Too Short to Box with God*. It's not that God gets angry and punishes those who ask questions; it's just that any God who is small enough to be scrutinized and judged by any of us wouldn't be God Almighty in the first place—or the Omnipotent or the Creator. Let me state it another way. The key assumption of the verse quoted to our blinded friend was that God works in everything for good—that is, God reserves the right to twist a blessing out of whatever cruelties are heaped on us as free moral agents.

On a Sunday some years ago, I preached on the stumbling enemy. I admitted that at times during my own suffering and my many hardships, I had wondered what God was thinking about. In such a context, however, we can ask God for wisdom about the weird behavior of our enemies or the sufferings we undergo, and God won't mind at all. Now I have come to see that unjust enemies never get away with their mischief. When they reach the point at which the harm might be too much, God lets something or somebody trip them up, and they do stumble and fall. I'm ready to trust my God now without ever wavering because my seventy-eight years have shown me that God is just and that I have nothing to fear.

It is amazing how God blesses trusting people with such awesome insights. I don't know how many times I have visited a saintly sister who was dying with cancer or some other incurable illness only to come away helped, when I had gone originally to help her! In each case, the blessed sister showed profound wisdom and great dignity even in such a potentially powerless and belittling process as dying. She transcended this circumstance by faith with no trace of doubt.

Too often, we put faith at one end of the spectrum and wisdom at the other. But faithful folk ask for wisdom, and they do get it. Thinkable faith does bring wisdom within reach. If you ask God for spiritual wisdom and ask in faith without doubt, you will receive it. I must not speak too loosely about doubt, however. There is such a thing as healthy doubt, an intellectual exercise of questioning that is the result of loving the God of truth with all our minds. Questions as to why we have to go through trials are sometimes called doubt, but God knows that we can't help wondering about hardships and wants us to think our way through our suffering with questions and whatever else it takes. God needs no protection from us. Therefore, we should encourage rather than squelch the questions of our children and of our own.

It may be difficult to separate the two, but intellectual curiosity is one thing, and spiritual doubt is quite another. Pat, simplistic answers about deeply spiritual issues are more dangerous than honest questions. Even the honest question Are you saved? is not that easy to answer. From the perspective of eternity, there are three different answers in three different time frames: I have been saved; I am being saved; and I will be saved. The old folks used to sing, "Have you got good religion?" And the answer was, "Certainly, Lord." But they also sang, "Pray for me." And they asked in their testimonies for us to pray that they might grow stronger. They also prayed that not a thing would come up in the judgment that might condemn them. It was a race that was not over yet. And it was a real race, so the finish was in some sense still undetermined. It is indeed a dishonest and unhealthy mind that has no questions.

Granting all this room for questions, however, does not make negotiable certainty about the goodness or providence of God. If you ask God for anything that is in God's will, it is a mockery for you to doubt the results. It has been said that if you pray for rain, you ought to carry an umbrella. God's timetable does not always match ours, but God will not withhold from us any good thing in due season. What is good and what is in season are determined by God, not by us.

James says in 4:3 that we ask and fail to receive because we ask amiss or we ask in error. Often it is because we ask for the wrong things. But when we ask for forgiveness with repentance, when we ask for salvation, when we ask for strength to be accountable, and when we ask for wisdom, we will receive, that is, if we ask in faith without a trace of doubt. It is in the very nature of things that we cannot receive that which we already believe to be in question.

Beloved, we are saved by grace through faith. We have no right to test God, so let us rejoice in the certainty that our God is good. Let us continue to enjoy the blessings of strength and wisdom that will be ours just for the asking. The eyes of the mind are made keen by the grace of our God, who only wants us to desire and pray for strength and wisdom. Pray in faith without a doubt.

The day of the notion that women are so trusting because we are intellectually inferior is over! And God has said through the Word that we can have spiritual wisdom if we ask in faith. Poor performances of our children in school can be overcome by faith and by prayers for our children. Moreover, we can pray that teachers will gain wisdom to be able to teach our children to read and to count so they can take part in the world of technology and sophisticated computers. The potential of our children defies the imagination. But we must teach all our children to pray for strength and wisdom with unwavering faith. Such prayer would affect not only how our children think of God but how they think of themselves and those around them. The problem of low self-esteem and self-confidence can be licked. We and our children can be spirit-filled living examples of trust without doubt.

This is no mirage, no empty dream. God has been giving men and women strength and wisdom to win and achieve from the time of creation. Through the years, people have convinced me time and time again that if you ask in faith believing, if you seek and do not doubt, after a while and by and by God will pour out blessings more than we can ever count.

On this day when we celebrate the gifts of women, let us look at some whose lives have been woven into the mosaic of *herstory*. God, the Mother/Father, was with our biblical as well as our ethnic ancestors, pushing them out into a chilly and nonreceptive world. These women moved with faith without a doubt, and God met them with all the resources of wisdom and courage to achieve their goals in life. God met Jochebed, Miriam, and Esther. God met Ruth, Deborah, Mary, Lydia, and Prisca, or Priscilla, as we remember her.

Some women have made a significant difference in our world: Lucy Laney, Mary McCleod Bethune, and Dolly Metz in the field of education; various missionaries to the Congo; Rachel Swann, Emily Gibbes, and Thelma Adair as pioneers in the national arena of the Presbyterian Church (USA). Thelma was the first African American woman to serve as the moderator of the General Assembly of the Presbyterian Church and of Church Women United. Presently on a tour of duty is Rebecca Winbush, who has served on the national staffs of many churches as well as Church Women United. Two among the womanist theologians of our day are Katie Canon, the first African American woman to be ordained in the Presbyterian Church (USA), and Delores Williams, an associate professor of theology at Union Theological Seminary. Too numerous to mention are "those preachin' women" of all denominations who have tested their faith without doubt.

I'm glad that our God has given these women of faith an opportunity to witness in causes of God's kingdom. I'm glad that their faith sustained them in the ups and downs of the struggle to serve in what appeared to be a man's world. I'm glad their prayers were made to our all-wise God, who never frowns at our questions and never censors our prayers. I'm glad that when they asked for wisdom and strength, they asked in faith without doubt. We are all blessed by their labors. Praise God!

7

Learning to Handle Our Midnight

Acts 16:25-31

Otis Moss Jr.

Learning to handle our midnight! Ponder this account from Acts 16:25: "And at midnight, Paul and Silas prayed, and sang praises unto God: and the prisoners heard them." Isn't that remarkable? At midnight, Paul and Silas prayed and sang praises. It's good to have a prayer partner. It's good to have a song. It's wonderful to know how to praise God. When you do that, you will get the attention of other people. Note that the prisoners listened to them.

You can handle daylight—when things are going well, when the lights are on, when the bills are paid on time, and when everybody is congratulating you. But can you handle midnight? You can handle daylight—when everybody tells you you're handsome, you're pretty, you're beautiful, you are somebody, you are the best, you are the greatest, that God was at his best when he made you. You can handle daylight—when there are no pains and no missed steps. But can you handle midnight—when the phone stops ringing, when the letters stop coming, when those who once said you were good-looking look the other way, when those who once

51

walked with you cross the street to the other side and pretend
they don't see you, when your best friend has forgotten your
address, and when the post office has canceled your zip
code? Can you handle midnight? You can handle daylight—
when you're young and energetic and you can climb the
steps, skip three, hit the middle, and then the top. But can
you handle midnight—when you have to take one step at a
time, when you have to pause halfway and catch your breath,
when you have to wait for another renewal of energy before
you can get to the top? We can handle daylight, but have we
learned to handle our midnight?

First, you need to be able to define midnight. Midnight is
a bridge between yesterday and tomorrow. In order to get
out of yesterday and step into tomorrow, you must pass
through midnight. Midnight is a bridge. You cannot move
from the world of yesterday across the world of today into
the world of tomorrow without some pain. We live, I think,
in three worlds: the world that was, the world that is, and
the world that is yet to be. You have to be able to appreciate
each world, for if you cannot appreciate yesterday, you don't
understand your roots. If you are not relevant today, you
cannot bear any fruit. And if you have no hope for tomorrow,
you cut off your future. We live in three worlds, and midnight
gets us out of an old world into a new one.

"And at midnight, Paul and Silas prayed, and sang praises
unto God: and the prisoners heard them." Now, if you cannot
handle midnight, you can't bear any fruit. Someone sent me
a poem several years ago that went something like this: "A
tree that never had to fight for sky, and air, and sun, and light,
but stood out in the open plain and always got its share of
rain, never became a forest king or queen, but lived and died
a shrubby thing." A tree that has never been in a storm is
dangerous to climb. You can't really trust such a tree because
its limbs are not dependable and the body of the tree is weak.
But a storm shakes a tree at its very foundation. When the
tree shakes, the ground around the roots loosens up, and the

roots go deeper. When the roots go deeper, the limbs stretch out, and while the limbs are stretching out, the top goes higher and higher. This means that the storm enables the tree to grow three ways at the same time: deeper, wider, and higher. So, if you run from, try to escape from, or deny your midnight, you cancel out your growth. It's a sin not to grow!

Yet we do attempt to avoid the storms and the midnights because we think midnight is a stumbling block. I have been taught that the only difference between a stumbling block and a steppingstone is how high you step! It might be that you have many stumbling blocks because you are not stepping high enough! Remember the words of the song: "Love lift me up where we belong, higher, higher, higher, higher."

Let's look at midnight in another way. I stood one day at the foothills of life, and I said to God, "Take away my pain and I will be happy." But God said to me, "If I take away your pain, I must also take away your gain. I must take away all of your spiritual progress. If I take away your pain, you cannot grow in grace." I said to God, "Then let me have my pain, but teach me how to bear it." I stood one day at the foothills of reality, and I said to God, "Take away my cross, and I will be happy." But God said to me, "Your crown is wrapped up, wrapped up in your cross, and when you bear your cross, you're just unwrapping your crown." I said to God, "A consecrated cross I bear until death shall set me free and then go home my crown to wear." I stood one day at the foothills of life, and I said to God, "Take away my tears, and I will have joy." But God said to me, "If I take away your tears, I must take away all of the prophets and the saints from around you. Not only that, I must take away Jesus, who did cry sometimes." I heard from God, and God told me, "I didn't give you tears to depress you, but I gave you tears that they might wash out your eyes and give you clearer insight and a more focused vision."

Midnight is sometimes crying time, but it is also vision

time. Midnight is sometimes a time of agony, but it is also strengthening time. Midnight is sometimes a lonely moment, but it is also a time when you can go "to the garden alone, while the dew is still on the roses," and hear the voice falling on your ear. Have you ever heard the voice of God?

"At midnight, Paul and Silas prayed, and sang praises unto God; and the prisoners heard them." If I could tune in on the wires of history, I would want to listen in on the conversation of Paul and Silas from sundown to midnight. I can imagine Paul saying, "You know, I didn't want to come here in the first place. I wanted to go to Bithynia, but somebody broke in on me at midnight and said, 'Come over to Macedonia.'" I can hear Silas saying, "You know, I would not be here if you hadn't brought me here. I was all right where I was." Between sundown and midnight, nobody came by to see about Paul and Silas. Lydia had joined the church, but she didn't come by. Between sundown and midnight, the NAACP didn't come by to file a writ of habeas corpus. Between sundown and midnight, SCLC didn't come by; it had not been organized. Between sundown and midnight, Amnesty International didn't come by; they were not on the scene. The ACLU didn't come by. The Thirteenth, Fourteenth, and Fifteenth Amendments to the Constitution didn't come by. The Bill of Rights didn't come by, and the missionary society didn't come by. But, about midnight, Paul and Silas prayed anyhow. I don't know what prayer Paul and Silas prayed, but if they had the language of our African American elders, they could have said:

> This evening, our heavenly Father, once more and again your humble servant is knee-bent and body-bowed. While I bow, I want to thank you for my last night lying down. The bed I rested on was not my cooling board, and the cover that I wrapped up in was not my winding sheet. You sent guardian angels to watch over me all night long while I slumbered and slept. Then early this morning you

touched me. (Have you ever been touched?) You touched me with a finger of love and woke me up in due time. I was yet left in a gospel land and a Bible-reading country where men and women won't do right. Lord, while I bow, please search my heart. If you find anything lurking around and about in it, like sin or hatred, move it as far as the East is from the West into the sea of forgetfulness where it will always go downward, never to rise against us anymore in this world nor to condemn us at the judgment bar. Lord, when it's your time to call and my time to answer, come on in a dying room; make old death behave. Come so close I can lean my head on your breast and breathe my life out sweetly there. Then take me over yonder where Job said the wicked will cease from troubling and the weary will be at rest, over yonder where it's always howdy, howdy and never goodbye, over yonder where every month is the month of May, every year is the year of jubilee.

They prayed and they sang and the prayers went up. Hallelujah! You don't mind if I tell it just like I feel it. The prayers went up to the throne of grace and fell at the mercy seat, and God said, "My servants are having a prayer meeting at midnight; my servants have organized a choir in the jailhouse at midnight. I want to talk to the earthquake and give an assignment to the earthquake. Some people have an earthquake; some have a faithquake, but the earthquake got an assignment."

Let me tell you, it was not a major earthquake. It was a minor earthquake with a major mission. It was not a major earthquake; it didn't harm the jail. It just shook it and opened the doors. It was not a major earthquake; it did not leave grounds to collect on the insurance policy. It was just a minor earthquake, but it cut loose the bands. Everybody's bands were loosed, and all the doors were opened. Paul and Silas got up and opened the doors of the church because somebody said, "What must I do to be saved?" Paul said, "Believe in Jesus."

We were in a prayer meeting, and now it's a church meeting. Not only is it a church meeting, it's a revival meeting. Come to Jesus just as you are. Come on anyhow. Come and go with me to my Father's house. I don't know what your midnight might be, but you ought to have a prayer, ought to have a song, ought to have some love in your heart. If you have a song in your soul, love in your heart, prayer in your view, you can handle your midnight.

When midnight is over and the sun begins to rise, you can tell the world, "I'm free at last," tell the world, "I know somebody who lifted my burdens! I know somebody who wiped tears from my eyes! I know somebody who's a mother for the motherless, a father for the fatherless!" I know somebody, and he's been good to me.

When I was a little boy of ten years, I made my vow to the Lord, and I'll never turn back. I know something about God. God put me through college on the installment plan and put me through seminary on a crust of bread and a glass of water! I know something about God. Since I was four years old, God has been my mother! Since I was sixteen, God has been my father! I know my God is a rock in a weary land and a shelter in the time of a storm. In the midnight hour, God will teach you how to handle your midnight and lead you into "the rising sun of a new day begun."

8

How to Get Out of Hell

Jonah 2.1 10

James C. Perkins

The religious experience of our generation has been seriously impoverished as a result of our tragic failure to believe in the haunting reality of hell. Claiming to be intellectually superior to our foreparents, we have dismissed the doctrine of the brimstone and the fiery pit as nothing more than a frightening, fabricated fairy tale woven of gossamer. A silent consensus that views hell as an invention of the pulpit seems to have emerged. The word has been whispered from person to person, from pew to pew, and from place to place that hell is an allegory invented by pulpiteers of other days for the purpose of frightening us out of enjoying the pleasures of life for the more nebulous experience of "serving the Lord."

Yet as neat and convenient as such an explanation may sound, there is no escaping the fact that hell is more than a scare tactic. Whether or not we believe in hell as a fact of the afterlife, with all manner of nefarious activity occurring around us, there just is no disputing that hell is a horrible fact of this life. Whatever we may believe about hell in our personal faith system, hell is certainly no figment of the prophetic imagination! Hell is a reality!

The preaching and theology of our foreparents placed
more emphasis on the judgment of God than do the theology
and preaching of our time. Our ancestors believed in a cosmic
battle between good and evil! They believed in the devil and
hell! They believed that God would reward the righteous
and punish the evildoer! And it seems that this spiritual
perspective created within them a deeper reverence for God
and life.

When our forebears spoke of heaven and hell, we ridiculed
them and accused them of being otherworldly. But otherworldly or not, at least they had enough sense to see that a
divine law of judgment is built into the very nature of life.
They knew that no matter who you are, in this world you
reap what you sow! You get back what you give! What goes
around comes around! What goes up will surely come down!
They understood that you experience the fiery fingertips of
hell simply by experiencing the consequences of your own
evil actions!

Suddenly we have become so sophisticated that we claim
our spiritual sensibilities are offended by any reference to
such realities as sin and judgment, as the devil and hell! We
contend that what we need is, not judgment, fire, and brimstone, but a positive message that teaches us positive principles to induce positive thinking to inspire positive living!
Despite all our positive thinking, the devastating effects of
sin and the scorching proof of hell are still all around us.

The religious experience of our time is shortchanging us
because it is missing the grave accent of the judgment of
God. It's telling us all about the boundless blessings of God!
It's telling us all about the precious promises of God! But it
is not telling us that "the soul that sinneth . . . shall die"
(Ezekiel 18:20). In consequence, we are not taking seriously
the judgment of God or the consequences of our own actions.
We are living as though we can act any way we please and
do anything we please without having to answer to anybody!
And the result is that we have made an infernal mess of our

lives! Our wild, undisciplined, unethical, irreverent lifestyles have turned our communities into the outskirts of hell.

Yes, more than we, our foreparents stressed the judgment of God and the reality of hell! And some of us are alive today because they did. Some of us have been spared needless pain. Some of us avoided an early grave. Some of us missed a whole lot of hell in life because we were taught that "the fear of the LORD is the beginning of wisdom" (Proverbs 9:10)

No matter what we say, hell is not just a damnable, unfortunate set of circumstances that we wake up and find ourselves in. Hell is a circumstance that we create for ourselves. When we live our life with no regard for the judgment of God, we're headed for hell! When we act but fail to consider the consequences of our actions, we're headed for hell! When we think only of pleasing ourselves with no thought that our pleasure may be causing somebody else some pain, we're headed for hell! Hell is not just a place of punishment after we die. If we ignore God and disregard his divine law of reciprocity, we'll end up creating our own private hell!

No, there is no need to think of hell as only an experience of the afterlife. Hell is a fact of this life! All across our world, there are diabolical conditions that trap and torture human life in the red-hot flames of hell! Every second of every minute of every hour of every day, some people are living through a form of torture, misery, or pain! From those kept suffering by the satanic systems of this world to the crack-addicted babies born in the ghettos, many people have lives singed entirely by the licking, laughing flames of hell! It's hell to have to live in squalor when wealth and affluence are teasingly dangled before your wanting eyes! It's hell to have to walk dangerous streets overcrowded with dope fiends, cutthroats, and back stabbers! It's hell to live in a so-called land of opportunity and yet be unable to find even a summer job!

No, there is no need to think of hell merely as an apocalyptic,

eschatological cauldron sitting on a big gas range at the South
Pole of eternity. There are pockets and outposts of hell all
around us. Hell is the situation in which women are physically and mentally abused by the demonized men in their
lives! Hell is the situation in which innocent children are
maimed and murdered by persons whose souls have been
satanized! Hell is the situation that tortures before it destroys.
Hell is the situation from which there seems to be no exit!

No matter what the circumstance, we always need a way
out! We always need the blessing of moving on to the next
experience! We always need to know that deliverance is a
possibility! When we know that we're not stuck, we can
endure any pain! We can face any foe! We can handle any
hardship! We can survive any fiery trial if we know that
there is a way out!

Some people have been in a hellified situation for so long
that they have become hopeless about their lives, concluding
that there's no way out! This is at least one reason it pays to
be serious-minded when you come to church. Church might
be a joke to you! Church might be an extension of your
weekend entertainment! But there are some people for
whom church is spiritual survival! Some people are on a
two-hour furlough from hell, and they come to church looking for a way out! Some people are AWOL from hell, and
they slip away to the church looking for a way out! And the
good news is that no matter how you get in hell, there is a
way out!

Ask the prophet Jonah. He landed in hell, but he'll tell
you that there is a way out! As a prophet of God, Jonah
should have known that hell was his destination when he
disobeyed God's orders and tried to do things his way. I
don't know what went through Jonah's mind when the angel
came and announced that Jonah was to be the guest preacher
for the first citywide revival service to be held in the sinful
city of Nineveh! But for some reason, Jonah decided he didn't
want to go. He hated the Ninevites. He didn't want them to

be saved. He decided that if the Ninevites were to be saved
it wouldn't be under his preaching. Jonah said to himself,
"Now I love to preach, but if God plans to save those sinful
Ninevites, he'll have to get himself another preacher, because
I'm going on vacation." It's a hellish attitude to want God
to bless only us and the folks we like!

And the word is that Jonah went down to Joppa, pur-
chased a ticket to Tarshish, and paid the fare. You know, a
ticket to hell is very expensive! Sometimes it costs health
and strength! Sometimes it costs an arm or a leg! Sometimes
it costs an eye or a kidney! Some people have paid as much
as their sanity! Some people have paid as much as their
family! And some people have paid as much as their very
life! A ticket to hell costs an awful lot! I don't know exactly
how much it costs, but I do know that it's more than I've
got, and it's more than you can afford!

Jonah paid the price thereof! He thought he had won this
tug of war with God. God said, "Nineveh!" Jonah said,
"Tarshish!" God said, "Nineveh with its sinful streets!" Jonah
said, "Tarshish with its white sandy beaches!" God said,
"Nineveh with its lustful lifestyle!" Jonah said, "Tarshish
with its refreshing breezes!" God said, "Nineveh with its
wretched conditions!" Jonah said, "Tarshish with the shade
of its palm trees!"

Trying to escape the presence of the Lord, Jonah went to
Tarshish. Now, the only place you can go to try to get away
from God is hell! I don't care how good it looks or what a
popular hot spot it is; if you're trying to get away from God,
that place is hell! The name on the map might say Tarshish!
The name on the map might be New York! The name on the
map might be somebody's house! But wherever you go
trying to escape the presence of the Lord, that place is hell!
Jonah boarded a ship to go to Tarshish, and he ended up in
hell. He should have had sense enough to know that even
in hell he couldn't get away from God, for as the psalmist

tells us, "Even if I make my bed in hell, behold, thou [God] art there" (Psalm 139:8).

The next part of Jonah's story is familiar. There was a storm. Cargo was thrown into the sea. Jonah slept. The sailors cast lots. The lot fell on Jonah, who was cast overboard. But God had prepared a great fish, and that fish consumed Jonah in the bowels of hell! Jonah tried everything he could to get out on his own. Jonah twisted! Jonah turned! Jonah squirmed! Jonah waited! Jonah hoped! He thought time would bring about a change! But when he recognized that he couldn't get out from the depths of hell on his own, Jonah cried unto the Lord, and the Lord heard his cry!

Pray Your Way Out

If you're in hell and you've had enough, there is a way out! To get out, first, you must pray your way out. From the lips of Jonah come these words: "Out of the belly of hell cried I, and thou heardest my voice" (Jonah 2:2).

Let's back up for just a moment. The first thing we do when we want to fling off moral restraint and head out of the presence of the Lord en route to our own Tarshish is to stop praying! The first step to hell is to stop talking to the Lord! Look back over your life, and you'll see that you started slipping when you stopped praying! Prayer is a way that you allow your life to stay under the control of God! The more you pray, the more control you allow God to exercise in your life! The less you pray, the less God can do with you! At some point, Jonah must have stopped praying. And doing so made it easy for him to reject God's orders! Even after the fish consumed him, Jonah was still too stubborn and hard-headed and hard-hearted and full of hell to pray right away! He was so mean-spirited that he would rather have died and been through with praying days! But God wouldn't let Jonah die! God wouldn't let him off the hook that easy!

Jonah couldn't get out of hell on his own! And you can't get out of hell on your own! Smarts won't get you out! Good contacts won't get you out! Consolidating all the bills won't get you out! You have to pray to get out of hell! Jonah tried everything he could, but nothing worked! Finally, Jonah opened his mouth and cried unto the Lord! He *cried* unto the Lord! In other words, he was desperate! He didn't just pray; he cried. And the tense of the verb indicates that Jonah kept on crying. In other words, his wasn't one of those little "lick and a **promise**" prayers. Jonah was wailing and soul travailing with God in prayer!

At first, Jonah got no answer! When you're in hell and trying to pray, it seems useless! From hell, God seems so far away! A prayer from hell is the ultimate long-distance phone call! But when you're in hell, you've got to keep on praying until God answers back! Jonah kept on crying unto the Lord, and the Lord called back! God said, "I hear you, Jonah. Where are you?" Jonah said, "I'm on my knees! " God said, "That's just where I've been trying to get you!"

If you're in hell, get on your knees! If you want out, get on your knees! You've got to pray your way out! Call the Lord! God will hear you! There's mercy with God! There's forgiveness with God! There's deliverance with God! There's a future with God! If you want out of hell, you've got to pray your way out!

Worship Your Way Out

The first step in the direction of hell is to stop praying. And the second step on that downward staircase to nowhere is to stop worshiping! Not only had Jonah stopped praying, but evidently at some point he had forsaken the temple. Maybe he though the temple was dull! Or maybe he viewed the temple as full of hypocrites! Or maybe he thought he was pretty good on his own without the temple. We don't know why Jonah stopped worshiping, but we do know that from the depths of hell he took another look. Jonah said, "I will look again toward thy holy temple" (2:4b).

The temple is not just a formality! The temple is a saving

force in your life! The temple is another way of staying in touch with God! If you're going to find God anywhere, you can rest assured that you will find God in the temple. As the prophet Habakkuk tells us: "The Lord is in his holy temple: let all the earth keep silence before him" (2:20). People who frequent the temple learn how to deal with the hell in their lives. Hell may break out all around them, but the temple is a refuge in the midst of hell, a shelter in a time of storm, a rest stop for the weary, a refueling station for sagging spirits.

While Jonah was in hell, he had time to think! He began to rethink the value and the place of the temple in his life! His past temple-going days ran through his mind! He said to himself, "When I went to the temple, my steps were steady! I had stability in my life! I felt better about myself! I had a hopeful outlook on my situation! I had joy in my heart!" Perhaps Jonah remembered these words of the psalmist: "I had rather be a doorkeeper in the house of my God, than to dwell in the tents of wickedness" (Psalm 84:10).

If you think the temple is irrelevant, if you think you can take or leave the temple, get in hell! From hell, the temple doesn't look so bad! In hell, Jonah started thinking. The temple crossed his mind! He promised God, "If you let me out of here, I'll sacrifice with the voice of thanksgiving!" In other words, Jonah said, "I'll praise your name! When I went to the temple before, I used to just sit there like a knot on a log. But if you'll let me out, I'll praise your name! When I went before, I didn't understand why people made all that noise. But if you'll let me out, I'll make a joyful noise! When I went before, I used to go just to go. But if you'll let me out, I'll have a testimony!" Jonah said, "I will pay that that I have vowed." In other words, he said, "I'll commit myself! I used to just have my name on the roll, but if you'll let me out, I'll commit myself! I'll pay my tithes! I'll be involved! I'll give my service! I'll worship you with my whole heart!"

If you want to get out of hell, you've got to worship your way out, praise your way out, give your way out, sing your way out, serve your way out, shout your way out. Worship will keep you out of hell! And worship will get you out of hell.

Trust Your Way Out

From the depths of hell, Jonah prayed to get out. He promised the Lord that once he was free, he'd go back to the temple. Jonah did everything he could do. But finally after he had done all, Jonah simply had to wait and trust God to let him out! He had to learn the lesson that "salvation is of the Lord" (Jonah 2:9).

You can get yourself into a hell of a mess, but salvation is of the Lord! Your friends and family can make your life hell, but salvation is of the Lord! You can get yourself in, but you and nobody else can get you out, for salvation is of the Lord! The best lawyer in the world can't argue you out! The best doctor can't write a prescription so you can medicate your way out! The best banker can't loan you enough money to buy your way out! The best psychiatrist has no word of wisdom in his therapeutic arsenal to counsel you out! The shrewdest legislator can't pass any law to force you out! The union can't organize a protest and demand that you be let out! The preacher can pray for you, but he can't pray enough to pray you out! Salvation is of the Lord!

You see, once you're in hell, you're on a when-God-gets-ready schedule! And God may not be ready until you've learned your lesson! God may not be ready until you're more humble in spirit! God may not be ready until you know how to treat your fellow person! God may not be ready until you act like you've got the sense he gave you! God may not be ready until you've changed your evil ways! God may not be ready until you make a commitment to serve him! When you get in hell, you can't get out just because you want to! You may want out, but you've got to wait until God is ready!

Hell can't do anything without God's permission! Hell might swallow you up, but it can't destroy you if God's not finished with you! If you'll pray, if you'll worship, if you'll trust, after awhile God will be ready, and he will let you out!

Jonah had done all he could do. Now he just sat there in that hell of a situation and just trusted and waited on God! After awhile, God decided that Jonah had suffered long enough! He spoke to the fish, and it spit him out on dry land!

If you'll trust God, he'll speak to whatever has a grip on your life, and God will set you free! If you'll trust God, he'll speak to your binding demon, saying, "Loose him and let him go. Loose her from the chains of an inferiority complex that shackle her mind. Loose him from the ropes of wretchedness that bind his soul! Loose her from the bondage of hate that fills her heart! Loose him and let him go!" No matter how hellified the situation, if you'll pray, if you'll worship, if you'll trust, God will deliver! For salvation is of the Lord!

9

God Hears the Pray-er

Luke 10 10 11

Jini Kilgore Ross

People of all generations have wanted to know how to pray. Indeed, the disciples asked Jesus to teach them to pray, and Luke presents the model prayer—the Lord's Prayer—as a response to their request (Luke 11:1-4). In my own Christian sojourn, I've heard many prescriptions for prayer.

If we're going to pray and pray right, we're told to "pray the Word." That's the current thinking. In her book *How to Pray for Your Children*, author Quin Sherrer from Women's Aglow Ministries has found all of the verses from the Bible that deal with children and offers these verses as prayers to use for various situations that we encounter with our sons and daughters.[1] "Just pray the Word," the proponents of this teaching tell us. "God will honor his Word," they say. Others, just as well-meaning, say that we need the baptism of the Holy Spirit, which, according to their theology, has been confined to speaking in tongues. They believe that this is the meaning of Romans 8:26-27, which says that the Spirit intercedes in praying for us with groanings too deep for words. If we pray in tongues, they say, our prayers will, without any effort on our part, be in direct line with the will of God, and

it will be in a language that the devil can't understand. All
we need is the baptism of the Holy Spirit.

But what is prayer, really? There are at least two ways to
define something: by synonym and negation. Clement of
Alexandria, a second-century church patriarch, defined
prayer as "conversation with God." A French proverb de-
fines prayer as "a cry of hope." Negation tells us what prayer
is not, as in "Prayer is not a formula."

Prayer Is Not a Formula

The problem with prescriptive thinking, such as in "Pray
the Word" and "Pray in tongues," is that it reduces prayer to
a formula. If prayer were a formula, then Jesus would not
have rebuked the Pharisees who were applying their for-
mulas in prayer. The text in Luke 18:11-12 shows one Pharisee
as saying the right things: "'God, I thank Thee that I am not
like other people: swindlers, unjust, adulterers, or even like
this tax-gatherer. I fast twice a week; I pay tithes of all that I
get'" (NASB). But his heart was not right. First of all, he was
self-righteous, judging himself better than others because of
his inflated estimation of himself. Secondly, Jesus taught his
disciples not to stand and pray in the synagogues and on the
street corners in order to be seen by others, as the hypocrites
did (Matthew 6:5). This Pharisee was doing just that and
perfectly fit Jesus' description of a hypocrite.

Lest we think that we are better than the Pharisees, let's
remember that all of us who are engaged in organized religion
with its traditions and its rituals are in danger of becoming
like the Pharisees, for they were people who worshiped their
religion more than the God of their religion. For example, the
Pharisees were more concerned about taboos against certain
types of work on the sabbath than they were about doing
good when an opportunity to do so presented itself. Jesus
enjoined them by saying, "The sabbath was made for man, and
not man for the sabbath" (Mark 2:27).

But it's not just the Pharisees. Pastor J. Alfred Smith Sr.

once said in a sermon that so many folks start off worshiping the Lord but end up worshiping the church and their religious practices. Some folks just have to have a certain type of music to worship. In many, if not most, churches, only a certain type of dress is acceptable. In fact, in the not-too-distant past, women were not allowed to worship in pants. We practice pharisaism when we're more concerned about our traditions than we are about God's truths. We practice pharisaism when we're more concerned about how we say a prayer than we are about the heart and meaning of the prayer. That's a good definition of pharisaism. And it is something about which we all need to be cautious. Prayer is more than a formula.

Prayer Is More Than a Tradition

In *The Prayer Tradition of Black People*, Harold A. Carter records several traditional types of prayers of the African American religious experience. One deacon at a camp meeting in 1928 in South Nashville, Tennessee, prayed this prayer:

> Almighty! And all wise God our heavenly Father! 'Tis once more and again that a few of your beloved children are gathered together to call upon your holy name. We bow at your foot-stool, Master, to thank you for our spared lives. We thank you that we were able to get up this morning clothed in our right mind. For Master, since we met here, many have been snatched out of the land of the living and hurled into eternity. But through your goodness and mercy we have been spared to assemble ourselves here once more to call upon a Captain who has never lost a battle. Oh, throw 'round us your strong arms of protection. Bind us together in love and union. Build us up where we are torn down and strengthen us where we are weak. . . .
>
> And now, Oh, Lord, when this humble servant is done down here in this low land of sorrow: done sitting down and getting up: done being called

everything but a child of God; oh, when I am done,
done, done, and this old world can afford me a home
no longer, right soon in the morning, Lord, right soon
in the morning, meet me down at the River of Jordan,
bid the waters to be still, tuck my little soul away in
that snow-white chariot, and bear it away over yonder in the third heaven where every day will be a
Sunday and my sorrows of this old world will have
an end, is my prayer for Christ my Redeemer's sake
and amen and thank God.

Let's be truthful. Many a saint from this era of praying and
many of us who have inherited the traditions of our elders
have felt that unless we could pray in this manner, with this
poetic language, that we did not know how to pray. How
many times have I heard people say that they couldn't pray
like Sister or Brother Prayer Warrior, who had the language
down pat! So when praying time comes, everyone waits for
the one who can talk the talk to pray.

But, as proud as we are of our traditions, we must not let
them take the place of our pureness of heart. Jesus said,
"Blessed are the pure in heart: for they shall see God" (Matthew 5:8). Jesus said this because prayer is more than an
incantation. I think of witches when I think of incantations. I
think of cults when I think of incantations. Incantations are
formulaic sayings and chants that supposedly reach the ears
of God. Many religions practice incantations, and only certain people know how to say the incantations correctly. But
our prayer is heartfelt. The words are less important to God
than the sentiment behind them.

Ari L. Goldman, a religion reporter for the *New York Times*,
took a year's sabbatical from reporting to attend Harvard
Divinity School. He was nervous about attending because he
felt that as a marginal practitioner of Judaism, he was in
danger of being converted to Christianity at Harvard, which
he considered to be a great bastion of Christian doctrine. He
was a Jew by *tradition* who thought that Harvard would

epitomize the *zeal* of heartfelt Christianity. But he writes in his book *The Search for God at Harvard* that while he was exposed to the best in postmodern theological traditions— liberation theology, gay theology, and feminist theology—he was not once confronted with anyone who was zealous for a living Lord named Jesus Christ.[3] After a year at Harvard, he returned to his job and to his faith, determined to become a better Jew.

The Lord himself had something to say about the worship of traditions replacing true worship. He spoke it to John who was on the Island of Patmos, and John recorded it in the book of Revelation. The Lord's word to the church at Ephesus was that she had left her first love (Revelation 2:1-4). Good deeds and great traditions must not replace our first love, Jesus Christ, our Lord. It is Jesus, and not our traditions, that must be at the center of our faith, our worship, and our prayers.

God Hears the Pray-er

The renowned theologian Dr. Howard Thurman wrote in his book *Disciplines of the Spirit* that God hears the pray-er, the one who is praying.[4] Our words, said Thurman, are just symbols expressing the unutterable language of the heart. In our text from Luke 18, God heard both the Pharisee and the sinner, although the Pharisee would have been shocked to know that God heard the sinner because it was believed then, as it is believed by some now, that God only hears righteous people. But verse 14 tells us that God does, indeed, hear the sinner. If God did not hear the sinner, how would the sinner ever repent? God heard both the Pharisee and the sinner because, as Dr. Thurman said, "God hears the pray-er," the one who is praying.

God heard the Pharisee's prayer but did not answer him because God heard not only the words but also the heart of the Pharisee. And from that heart issued forth a formulaic prayer saturated through and through with self-exaltation

and self-righteousness. Jesus says in Luke 18:14 that self-exaltation does not stand up in the face of God. It has no place.

We are guilty of practicing self-exaltation. We exalt ourselves when we think that we're better than someone else.
We exalt ourselves when we congratulate ourselves for coming to church, paying our tithes, and doing God and humanity a favor. We exalt ourselves when we think that we're
superior because we made better choices in our youth than
someone else did or because we didn't succumb to the same
temptation that someone else did. We exalt ourselves when
we say that if others had chosen more wisely or resisted more
firmly, they wouldn't be in the shape they're in. When this
self-congratulatory spirit is operating in us, we might as well
skip the altar call because it will just be a meaningless,
ritualistic exercise unless we're there to repent.

A nation's prayers even fall on the deaf ears of God when
that nation blames her victims for their problems. As long as
America is tired of welfare recipients and bored with the homeless, as long as America's prevailing attitude is that these social
conditions constitute a drain on our economy and a blight on
our streets, as long as legislators in state after state and city after
city look for ways to rid themselves of these problems, then we
might as well call off the National Day of Prayer because God
isn't listening. We can't pretend that we're seeking solutions
when we really have attitudes of blame. We can't fool God with
the right words but the wrong spirit.

God hears the pray-er but turns a deaf ear to hypocritical
and self-righteous prayers. They aren't justified, as the Scripture says in Matthew 6:7, because prayer is a matter of the
heart and not the heaping up of "empty phrases" as the
Gentiles, or heathen, do. God heard the Pharisee but did not
bless the prayer. And God heard the sinner and blessed his
prayer. Why? For one thing, the sinner did not try to justify
himself before God. When we do that, we're playing God.
Only God can justify, that is, make us right or give us right
standing. There was no pretense with the sinner. He did not

try to bring God into a conspiracy of rationalization to excuse his sin. He didn't say, "I came from a dysfunctional family." He didn't say, "I was ostracized by my peers." He didn't say, "I had an emotional problem." No! Instead, he said, "God be merciful to me a sinner!" (Luke 18:13).

What wisdom the tax collector exercised in prayer. First, he recognized and appealed to God's nature and character, for the psalmist wrote that God's "mercy endures forever" (Psalm 107:1, NKJV). The Pharisee, despite all of his religious training, didn't seem to know enough about God to know that God despises self-righteousness. But the sinner knew that God could be merciful. Secondly, the tax collector knew enough to acknowledge and confess his true state, his sinfulness. His prayer was heard *and* answered because he prayed with a pure heart, according to God's precepts, when he sought mercy and confessed his sinfulness.

It's all right to pray God's Word, but it has no magic in and of itself unless your heart and faith are in it. It's all right to pray in tongues, but the Holy Spirit's intercession is not confined to those who do so. Many saints have lived and died without ever speaking in tongues, and God heard their prayers. It's all right to have a prayer tradition, but let it be a tradition of heart more than of tongue. Let it be a tradition of faith in God and belief in his Son for his Word rather than a tradition of the recitation of the words themselves. Let it be a tradition of humble submission to God's will in the same spirit that Jesus had when his own difficult hour came and he humbled himself and said, "Remove this cup from me: nevertheless not my will but thine, be done" (Luke 22:42).

God hears you and me, the pray-ers. And we ourselves, as we are in our hearts, are the substance of our prayers. Amen.

---

1. Quin Sherrer, *How to Pray for Your Children* (Lynnwood, Wash.: Aglow Publications, 1986).

2. Harold A. Carter, *The Prayer Tradition of Black People* (Valley Forge, Pa.: Judson Press, 1976), pp. 43-44.

3. Ari L. Goldman, *The Search for God at Harvard* (New York: Times Books/Random House, 1991).

4. Howard Thurman, *Disciplines of the Spirit* (Richmond, Ind.: Friends United Press, 1977).

10

Jesus Christ,
the Model Pray-er

Luke 11:1-18

Gary V. Simpson

Jesus Christ is the model pray-er. Indeed, Jesus is cast in this role in Luke 11:1: "And it came to pass, that, as he was praying in a certain place, when he ceased, one of his disciples said unto him, Lord, teach us to pray, as John also taught his disciples." The desire expressed in the words of the disciples as "Lord, teach us to pray" tells us plenty about the disciples and their Master-Teacher. Both student and teacher are acquainted with some tradition of prayer. After all, John the Baptist had been teaching his disciples to pray. Perhaps these students of Christ had watched John's protégés lift their hearts to God with such energy and power that they wanted the same substance to become a part of their Lord's training curriculum for disciples. Note, too, the disciples' belief that prayer is a learned activity.

We also discover in Luke 11:1 that Jesus is a praying man, for one cannot teach prayer if one does not practice prayer. The disciples' choral plea "Teach us to pray" is a testimony to their having seen Jesus pray. Jesus, being a partner-teacher, works with the disciples. Immediately after the disciples

reveal their hearts' desire to learn to pray, Jesus in the next
verse begins, "When you pray. . . ." Luke's account of the
Lord's model prayer then follows.

Let me suggest that Jesus did not teach the disciples to
pray only by the words in this text, for Jesus modeled prayer
in his lifestyle. He showed his disciples the posture of prayer,
the position of prayer. He showed them not only how to
pray but where to pray. Jesus showed them when to pray,
and why to pray. There are five points for us to examine

Prayer Is Power

Jesus understood prayer as power. Listen to what Jesus
says in Matthew 26:53 in the midst of his capture by enemies
on the dark night of his betrayal. One of Jesus' companions
had lifted his sword and struck the servant of the high priest,
cutting off that servant's ear. Jesus scolded the companion,
instructing him to put away the sword, for it was merely an
instrument of death. Matthew 26:52 expresses Jesus' reason
with these words: "They that take the sword shall perish
with the sword." But listen to what Jesus says about the
power of prayer in his next words to the zealous disciple:
"Thinkest thou that I cannot now pray to my Father, and he
shall presently give me more than twelve legions of angels?"
(verse 53).

Now, that's power! Jesus shows us that by talking to God
we have access to power. Someone has said, "No prayer, no
power. Much prayer, much power." Prayer is the fuel of our
ability. Just by asking God, Jesus declares, "I can call down
twelve thousand angels. I don't need disciples to defend me.
All I have to do is say to God, 'Send me twelve thousand
angels,' and they'll come immediately to my rescue or sit
right by my side." That's power.

We ought not pray if we do not believe that prayer is
power. If we think prayer is merely words we utter before
God, if we think it's just our laundry list of things we want,
if we think it's like a wish list for Santa Claus on Christmas,

then we have not discovered what Jesus has shown us about prayer. Prayer is power. When we ask God for something, we must believe that it shall be done.

You've got power today. Are you worried about your job? Are you worried about your home? Are you worried about the mean streets where you live? Are you worried about your church? Don't you know that prayer is power? You are sitting on dynamite. You have spiritual nuclear warheads in your bosom. If you just pray, you can bring the power of God to your attention. Prayer is power.

Prayer is not just asking God for something. It is a relationship with God. And through prayer, we abide in God. You and I through prayer call God into action. Did you know that? To be certain, we do not order God around through our prayers, for prayers do not change the essence of who God is. No matter how effective or effectual the prayer, we cannot pray more holiness into God. No matter how fervent the pray-er, we cannot pray any greater self-sufficiency in God. We cannot pray any more power into God, for God *has* that power. But God is waiting for someone to ask him to release that power on a specific problem. Prayers are our opportunity. Think about that. That's power. God made everything you see and everything that you cannot see millions and billions of miles into space. You can call that God into action for your particular needs. That's power. Right now, God is holding up the universe, and you have a chance to pull on God's coattail and say, "Don't forget about me; I need you in the midst of my life!" That's power!

Perhaps then, one reason why we are powerless is because we fail to realize the potential of power that rests in our bosom. You have power today. Irrespective of what people say to you, regardless of what the government may do, you have power in your bosom. God is still on the throne. When you do not pray about a concern, you may be the very hurdle over which God's answer cannot get. If you've got something in your heart today, something that's tearing away at the fabric of who you are; if you have something that beats you down, takes your energy, destroys your spirit, and depresses you; if you have something that you are holding on to that keeps you from realizing your potential, believe this: prayer is power.

Prayer Is Personal Business

Matthew 6:5-8 is this disciple's perspective on the circumstance of the Lord's model prayer. For Matthew, of course, the Lord's Prayer was a part of the Lord's magnum opus, his great work called the Sermon on the Mount. Before uttering the words of the prayer, Jesus teaches his disciples in verse 5 about the empty rewards of those who just stand up and pray on the corner of the street so people can say, "That's a great prayer. Look at that great man or woman of faith." Jesus said they had their reward. His words to his followers in verse 6 point them in a different direction: "But you, when you pray, enter into your closet. And when you shut the door, pray to your Father who is in secret. For the Father who sees you in secret shall reward you openly" (6:6, paraphrased). Prayer is personal business.

Verse 6 highlights the idea that prayer is a relationship with God. We do not have to air all of our personal business with everybody else. We can take the desires of our heart to God in prayer, shut the door behind us in a secret closet, and tell God all about it. We can sleep in confidence knowing that whatever we tell God will not be buzzing in the next day's "Do you know what I heard?" Prayer is personal business.

In Luke 11, we learn that Jesus "was praying in a certain place" (verse 1). And I like the way Luke says, "When he had finished praying, one of his disciples asked him, 'Lord teach us to pray.'" This disciple had learned that Jesus took prayer seriously. He knew when Jesus was sitting down in his "certain place" to pray that no one should interrupt that conversation between him and God. The disciple waited until Jesus had said his "Amen" to approach him.

So much of our prayer life is interrupted by things that don't matter, but talking to God is serious personal business. Amid the hustle and bustle of life, we need to shut down from the movement and shut out the windiness of life and its circumstances and be ushered into the presence of God in prayer. One does not have to have a crisis boiling over in one's life. In our world, just living takes a toll. It is inconsequential as to where we find ourselves on the ladder of success. One does not have to be up and in or down and out. Whether you are up or down, life takes a toll on you and me. Life dissipates our communion with God. It weakens our motives. It withdraws our gaze from God and places it on ourselves. Life puffs us up by conceit over our own power. Life weighs us down with the annoyance of resistance. Life depresses us with the consciousness and possibility of failure. Life makes war even on our religion in an attempt to waste it. We need some personal quiet space and time to talk to God about life.

A careful study of Jesus praying reveals not only that he withdraws to himself but also that he stays within eyeshot of his disciples. They could see the Savior kneeling and talking to God, but they could not hear what he was saying. People ought to catch you praying to God. Even if they don't know what you're saying, they ought to know that you have God in your life. Prayer is personal business.

Jesus reminds us that if we have personal business with God, we need to find the personal space into which we can go when we pray. We each need a prayer space, a closet. It doesn't have to be an actual closet, but we need to have some place where people will not disturb us, where we can feel the presence of God, where we can hear the voice of God. As we read in the psalm: "Be still and know that I am God" (Psalm 46:10). Prayer is personal business.

The things that are important and significant in his life

must be brought back to the Creator for advice, for guidance, and ultimately for submission to God's will. Prayer is personal business.

Prayer Must Include Others

Although prayer is personal business, Jesus reminds us that we have not finished our responsibility in prayer until we have also brought other people before God's presence. Although prayer is personal business, it is not selfish. If our prayers consist of "I" and "me" and "my" and "give to me" without an acknowledgment of all the other people who need things, who need the presence of God, then we waste our time.

In John 17, Jesus prays to God, and in the midst of that prayer he says, "I pray for them" (verse 9). The Jesus prayer is an acknowledgment that there are other people who need some of the power that prayer releases. Who are the ones Jesus prays for? We are the ones, the people who are in his name. In the same verse, Jesus says, "I pray not for the world, but for the people that you have given me, for they are yours" (paraphrased). Note that he was praying for other people who belong to God.

We cannot discover the full power of prayer without conscious, deliberate prayer for other people. If God does not answer your prayers about you, then perhaps you need to examine your prayers about others. If you want God to do something for you in your prayer life, then bring someone else who needs God's help into your prayer life and watch what God works for you. That's the way God works. God wants us to bring others in. By bringing others to God in prayer, we remind God that we are not in this thing by ourselves. This is why Jesus told his disciples, "When you pray, say: Our Father which art in heaven" (Luke 11:2, adapted). We must recognize that there are some other people praying to God right now whose needs are just as serious as ours, whose desires for God are just as real as ours, whose wants for God to speak and to move are just as important as ours. When we say, "our Father," we acknowledge that we are not the only one on the line.

In recent years, a new concept has swept across the telecommunications industry. In the wee hours of the morning, when loneliness often reigns, the television advertisers blitz the airwaves with a special appeal to remedy boredom and relieve loneliness. The pitch in that for a small fee (which is never really small) you can talk to a group of interesting and exotic people all across the country by just calling the party line. Twenty to twenty-five people from all over the country can talk to each other all at the same time. This was considered a revolutionary, innovative form of entertainment. When the party line was first introduced, this seemingly novel idea made millions of dollars for its advertisers. The truth is that here again we discover nothing new, for God has had a party line ever since prayer started. People can talk to God all at one time and at no time do you get shut out, does the busy signal buzz, does a recording politely request that you call back later because God is busy. God is *our* Father and can hear all our concerns at the same time.

If we think we are the only one talking to God, we cannot say, "our Father." We are not the only ones trying to get God's attention, and we must recognize even as we pray as a church that there are other churches in Jesus' name who need power, who need the presence of the Holy Spirit, who need the manifestation of love, peace, mercy, and grace. God is *our* Father.

Prayer Is the Main Business of the Church

By his actions in Matthew 21:12-13, Jesus shows us the seminal identity of the church. Jesus cast out of the temple those who sold and bought, the ones we call "the money-changers." Our Lord, in a fit of rage, threw them out of the temple, saying, "My house shall be called the house of prayer." Jesus, the model pray-er, shows us that prayer is the main business of the church. It is a natural tendency to look at Jesus' driving the moneychangers out of the temple as a specific action against them and their particular craftiness. But Jesus challenges us to see that these people could have been doing anything. They did not have to be exchanging money. Anything except the business of prayer keeps the church from fulfilling its original design and intent from God. We do not live up to our life as a church if it is not a house of prayer. Prayer is the main business of the church.

Jesus railed against the moneychangers with the words, "You have made [my house] a den of thieves" (Matthew 21:13). But the church does not have to be specifically a den of thieves to be guilty. It could be a den of liars, a den of gossips, a den of slanderers, a den of people organized just for social acumen. To be guilty, the church could be a place of class snobbery where the "who's who" get together and discuss their gratitude for not being the "who's not"! The church could be a den of anything. However, the primary business of the church is to be a house of prayer. If we come to church for any other reason, we do not live up to what God asks us to be, and we become "a den of thieves."

Perhaps some come to church just to be on the inside. Others come to be accepted by the people who count in society, thereby elevating their own status. If that is what the church has become, then it is not living up to its main business. If this is who we have become, Jesus stands on the outside of his own church with rage and judgment declaring, "You have made the church a den of something other than prayer." Prayer is the business of the church. Even when people come to church and cannot hear a good sermon, they ought to get a good prayer. If they cannot hear a good song, they ought to get a good prayer. For this is a house of prayer.

We sing in prayer. We preach in prayer. We testify in prayer. We shout in prayer. We read in prayer. This is a house of prayer. We give our offerings in prayer. We love one another in prayer. Our conversations should be in prayer.

Our exchanges should be in prayer. This is a house of prayer. If you and I cannot do anything else when we come to church, we can still pray. If you can't sing, pray. If you don't have a testimony, pray. This is a house of prayer.

Prayer Time Is High Time

In the Gospel of Luke, we read, "And it came to pass in those days, that he [Jesus] went out into a mountain to pray, and continued all night in prayer to God" (6:12). Jesus teaches us that prayer time is high time. Jesus "went out into a mountain," symbolizing that he was moving up from the mundane mire of the world. The Savior was stepping up into some holy ground. Christ stepped up into prayer. Prayer time is high time.

Although the posture of prayer is down on our knees, we can never rise to a higher posture than to go down in prayer in order that we might go up to the place of prayer in our hearts. Prayer ought to lift our spirits. It ought to encourage us. Prayer ought to give us some assurance that God has not left us by ourselves. Prayer brings us to the presence of God. It lifts the burdens off our backs. Prayer points us to the glorious will of God. Prayer brings earth's agenda into communion with heaven. Prayer seeks to raise our existence here to the presence of God there. Prayer opens up our access to the celestial legions of angels. Prayer puts us in touch with the one and only true God. Prayer carries our desires to the source of our lives. Prayer is like incense burning before the altar of God. Prayer time is high time.

Prayer gets God moving. Prayer calls God into action. Prayer ought to lift you up and let you know that God will not leave you nor forsake you. If you have a problem today, take it to God in prayer. A friend gave me good advice: "If you are going to worry, don't pray. If you are going to pray, don't worry." Watch how God will make you feel better and make you see that you are not in this thing alone. Prayer time is high time.

I discovered something this week. You know the old adage that says, "What goes up must come down." But prayer, through the divine power of the Holy Spirit, makes a difference. It inverts that scientifically verifiable axiom on its head, for prayer asserts the exact opposite: What goes down in prayer must come up. What goes down in prayer must come up in glory. What goes down in prayer comes up in power. What goes down in prayer comes up in might. What goes down in prayer comes up in Jesus' name. What goes down in prayer comes up before God. Prayer time is high time. Amen.

11

No Answer

I Kings 19:1-18

Jeremiah A. Wright Jr.

Effective praying involves a number of ingredients: praise, confession, contrition, thanksgiving, commitment, meditation (creative listening), intercession, and supplication. In this message, I want to examine the last of these: supplication, that is, praying for our own needs.

Supplication is an extension and amplification of the prayer breathing exercises espoused by Lloyd Ogilvie whereby we exhale saying, "Lord, I need you," and then inhale saying, "Lord, I receive you." Supplication, as the hymn writer William Walford phrases it, is that time during the "sweet hour of prayer" when we are bid at our Father's throne to make all our wants and wishes known. Supplication, praying for our own needs, is what draws us to where Elijah is in the wilderness, bearing his soul before God in prayer. "Lord, it's too much," he prayed in 1 Kings 19:4. "Take away my life. I might as well be dead. I can't stand it." "Lord," he prayed, "it's too much." This preacher, sitting there alone in the wilderness, utters a prayer that sounds so much like your prayers and like my prayers: "Lord, it's too much. I can't stand it."

Have you ever been alone in the wilderness? Sitting there

85

underneath a juniper tree, Elijah felt failure, fear, depression, worry, and hopelessness closing in on him. So he lay down and went to sleep. The preacher wanted to give up because things just weren't working right. Have you ever been there? And in Elijah's prayer life, unlike the great drama on Mount Carmel, we read in 1 Kings 19, there was silence. No answer came from God, the same God to whom Elijah had prayed, "O LORD, answer me, so that this people may know that you, O LORD, are God" (1 Kings 18:37 NRSV). No answer came from the same God who had responded on Mount Carmel by sending down fire from heaven, from the same God whose orders Elijah had been following, from the same God who had sent Elijah out to the brook Cherith, from the same God who had commanded the ravens to bring the prophet food. This same God is silent in chapter 19. There was no answer. Elijah prayed, "Lord, it is too much." There was silence—no answer. "Lord, I can't stand it." There was silence. "Lord, I have been trying to do what you told me to do, and look what it's gotten me." There was no answer.

In Elijah's prayer life, there was silence. No answer came from God. Now, I know some of you have been there. Members have asked me, "How come my prayers don't get answered?" As people have shared their pains and tears with me, they have said, "I hear all those wonderful things that people testify about saying how God answers their prayers, and I start to wonder what's wrong with me." What about all those times when prayer is unanswered? What about all those times you are waiting to hear from heaven and there's just no answer? What about all those times you poured out your heart in supplication, but it's not getting any better, and if anything, it seems to be getting worse? What about all those times the response to your prayer has been silence, no answer?

Consider the child who has gone bad, leaving a hole in your heart and an ache in your soul. And you have been earnestly and fervently praying in supplication asking God to at least do something about the pain, the gaping wounds that will not heal. And from heaven there has been no answer. Think of that job you cannot find. The Lord *knows* you need it to support your family. Now, I'm not talking about that job you are *not* looking for. You know, we've got some folks who are unemployed and aren't looking. They are waiting for a job to drop out of the sky into their laps. Other folks don't want a *job*, income for grits and greens, honest money for respectability and integrity. No, no. Those folks don't want a *job*; they want a *position*. No grits and greens for them; they want caviar and cognac. I'm not talking about either one of these folks. I am talking about folks looking for anything decent, and a job is just not to be found. In the meantime from the throne of grace, there has been no answer.

Consider that loved one of yours who's sick, that cancer in your own body, that habit you just can't break, that devastating death, that Christian mate you've been asking God about, that dark secret shared only between you and God, that unreconcilable ruptured relationship, that anger and bitterness eating away at your spirit, that loneliness dogging your every step. Consider those tears that you can hide from everybody else but Jesus. Consider whatever petition has poured out of the depths of your being in supplication and has caused you to say, "Lord, it's too much. I can't stand it." You know what those petitions are in your own life. You also know that in response to the specificity of your supplication, there has been silence. No answer. In fact, there have been times—and somebody right now feels this way—when you felt like giving up. There have even been times when you've felt like giving up on the practice of prayer. Be honest with yourself!

Well, what about those prayers for which you feel there has been no answer? What about those times, even in your practice of prayer, when you have felt like giving up? That's where Elijah is when we join him twenty miles deep in the wilderness. He prayed fervently, and there was no answer.

88

Jeremiah A. Wright Jr.

So he lay down and went to sleep. "Lord," we pray, "it's too much. I might as well be dead."

Job asked the same question we ask: "Who is this who hides counsel without knowledge?" (Job 42:3, NKJV). In our twentieth-century language, we ask, "Who is this who withholds answers to our prayers without purpose?" If you read the book of Job and hold it up against 1 Kings 19 and put your own life on both pages, several important insights emerge. Let me share just three with you.

The first insight is that all prayers are answered. Job had his prayer answered. God granted him a private interview, but the *interviewer* turned out to be the *interviewee*. Job thought he had some tough questions for God, but when the interview took place, God had some tougher questions for Job: "Where were you when the morning stars sang together?" (38:7). God had some much tougher questions, but Job's prayer was answered.

Elijah had his prayer answered. An angel woke him up, touched him, and said, "Get up!" (1 Kings 19:5). All prayers are answered. In our own lives, we must recognize that all prayers are answered. Remember, however, there is a big difference between unanswered prayer and ungranted petitions. Wishing is not real praying. Elijah said he *wished* he were dead.

Now, we can go to the throne of grace, make all of our wants and wishes known, have all of our wants granted, have all of our wishes granted, and still not have received an answer to prayer. Think about that!

The purpose of prayer is communion and conversation with God. The period of waiting for the granting of some request is often rewarded by a far greater gift than what we asked for. What gift is that? It is the gift of the Lord himself. That's what Job got. That's what Elijah got. And that's what we will get if we continue in prayer, realizing that all prayers are answered and remembering there is a difference between unanswered prayer and ungranted petitions. The prayer is answered, but the request is denied or delayed in some instances. And in those instances, what is delayed or denied is according to a much greater plan and wisdom than we can possess or fathom in our finite perception.

Brother Oswald Chambers put it something like this: Our understanding of God—that's the answer to prayer. Getting things from God—that's God's indulgence of us. When God stops giving us things, he brings us into the place where we can begin to understand him.

If we can get from God everything that we ask for, we will never get to know God. We look to him as a blessing machine, sort of a sanctified Santa Claus, blessing capitalism and a philosophy of prosperity. But when we have a dry spell like Elijah had—a dry spell when all we hear is silence from heaven, no answer to our specific supplication—a dry spell when it appears as if God has departed from us—when we have a dry spell, it is a sure sign that we are on the verge of a new depth in our relationship with the Lord. The purpose of so-called unanswered prayer or delayed or denied petitions is to lead us like Job or to lead us like Elijah from the hearsay of a Mount Carmel to the "heart sight" of a Mount Sinai.

Job said, "I have heard of you by the hearing of the ear" (Job 42:5, NRSV), but that is hearsay. He goes on, "But now my eye sees"; that is "heart sight." We say that God is love, but it is not enough just to *say* so, we have got to *know* so. We must know that God is love, and to know that, we must know God. God will use a dry spell to make us know him and to desire him more than the specific thing we have been praying for. Sometimes we want what we have been praying for more than we want God.

There is a terrible misuse of prayer that we practice so often. It happens when we use prayer as a manipulative device to get what we want when we want it. Prayer then becomes a substitute for the Lord himself. And when we start doing this, God always delays what we think is best for us until we want him more than we want an answer according to our specifications.

Do you know what I mean? Many of us know we need the Lord's help, and we want the Lord's help, but we don't know how much we need the *Lord*. When we don't get what we asked for, we're through with God. Ask yourself these personal questions. What happens when that marriage you have been praying about fails? What happens when that child you've been praying about doesn't get any better? What happens when that job you've been looking for, honestly been looking for for six months or a year, doesn't materialize? What happens when your loved one who is sick doesn't get any better? What happens when that cancer in your body doesn't go into remission? When that cancer metastasizes? When you don't find that Christian mate? You fill in the blanks. You know your own personal needs, your own personal requests. If it doesn't happen, the question is Will you still want God for God? Or do you just want to use God as a means for something else that you want?

Sometimes the request is denied, and sometimes the request is delayed, but the prayer is answered. All prayer is answered. And keep in mind this footnote. Sometimes a request is delayed because we are not ready to receive what God is willing to give. Sometimes we pray for things that are not best for us. Sometimes we pray for things that are not in keeping with the Lord's timing for us. But the point is this: do not give up on God because God doesn't give you what you want when you want it. There was an old black preacher named Charles Tindley in the city of Philadelphia, where I grew up, and he used to write hymns. And in his hymn "We'll Understand It Better By and By," which I used to hear as a little boy, he captured this thought poignantly:

Trials dark on ev'ry hand and we cannot understand
All the ways that God would lead us to that blessed
*   Promised Land;*

But He guides us with His eye and we'll follow till we die.
For we'll understand it better by and by.
By and by when the morning comes,
When the saints of God are gathered home,
We'll tell the story how we've overcome;
For we'll understand it better by and by.

If your prayer life is drawing you closer to God, helping you to build a consistent and abiding relationship with God, more than giving you a response to your specific demand, if it is enabling you to want and need God just because he is God and not for what you can get out of the deal, then your prayers are being answered, even though they seem like they are not. The first insight from the passage about Elijah is that all prayers are answered, and there is *contact*. Contact is made whenever you pray. God is not off on a vacation somewhere with the throne of grace put on hold until he comes back. When you pray, contact is established. The angel touched Elijah and said, "Get up." Contact was made.

The second insight has to do with *contour*, that is, the shape of the answer. The response to your prayer does not always come in the way you expect it to come. The shape (contour) may be different than what you expected. Job wanted an answer; that's what he prayed for. What he got was a response to his prayer, a long list of questions, a better understanding *of* God, a closer relationship *with* God, and more blessings than he'd ever dreamed of. The response didn't come the way Job expected it to come.

Elijah prayed to die: "Lord, it's too much. I can't stand it. Take away my life. I might as well be dead." The answer he received took a different shape: "Get up and eat" and again "Get up and eat; you have a long walk ahead of you" (1 Kings 19:5,7, NRSV, paraphrased). Look in verses 11-12. The answer Elijah got took a different shape from the one he expected: "Go out and stand on the mountain before the LORD" (NRSV). The Lord passed by and sent a furious wind, but God wasn't in the wind. The wind stopped blowing after splitting hills and shattering rocks, and then there was an earthquake, but God was not in the earthquake. The answer was not in the form that Elijah anticipated. After the earthquake, there was a fire. That was how God had answered on Mount Carmel, but here on Mount Sinai the answer was taking a different form because God was not in the fire. But after the fire, there was a still small voice. The answer did not come in the shape Elijah anticipated.

You see, Elijah prayed as we pray. His supplication was like ours. Elijah had something he wanted the Lord to do for him. And when we pray in supplication, we have something we want the Lord to do for us. But prayer is not only what the Lord does for us but what God wants to do through us. And God had something that he wanted to do through Elijah. The shape of the answer, the contour, was different than Elijah expected. He asked for God and got an angel. He asked for death; he got food and drink. He asked for some relief; he got a forty-day march in the wilderness. He expected a mighty roar from Zion; he got a still small voice. He expected some sympathy and a leave of absence; instead he got some marching orders and a new assignment. First Kings 19:15-18 shows us that the response to our prayers doesn't always come in the way we expect it to come.

The first insight has to do with *contact*. The second insight has to do with *contour*, the shape or form in which the answer comes. The third insight has to do with *content*—what God says in response to our prayers.

Let me introduce content through a personal experience. Sometimes you and I get confused the way Elijah got confused. We want to please people instead of pleasing God. And let me tell you one thing about people: they will always leave you in a constant state of fear. We're afraid we will not please this one. If we please this one, we're afraid we will not please that one. People pleasers are always afraid. You know, I used to be a people pleaser. When I first started pastoring here at Trinity, eighteen months into my service of ministry, it seemed as if everyone was leaving. The music I introduced was wrong. The hymnbooks we bought were wrong. My sermons about black folk and racism and systemic evil and about what God was saying and doing with his people in the 1970s—all of that was wrong, and everybody was leaving. I was upset and afraid. Like Elijah, I said, "Lord, it is too much."

I ran, not into the wilderness, but to see the founding pastor of this church, the Reverend Kenneth B. Smith. I poured out my heart to Ken; I told him how I was feeling and failing and that it was not working. And I felt I owed him an apology and an explanation because, after all, he had started this work, and I was afraid I was killing it. My prayers were not being answered, so it seemed. I was miserable. Dr. Smith pointed out to me that I was taking my signals from the wrong source. I was into people pleasing so deeply that I was missing what God was doing, the content of his response.

Ken asked me, "How many members have left, Jerry?" I said, "I don't know; it seems like everybody." He said, "Let's count them." He pulled out one of our old church directories. We went through the directory and came up with 22 names. Then he said, "How many have joined since you've been there?" I said, "I don't know." When you're down, everything is distorted, and you can't see anything clearly. Ask Elijah. He said, "Let's count them." Ken pulled out the annual report from my first year as pastor, and 66 had joined. We called back to the church and checked with the secretary and found that in the first nine months of 1973 60 more had joined. And he said, "My brother, don't ignore the 120 that God has sent you worrying over the 22 who have left you. You can't be everybody's pastor. You can't please everybody. Concentrate on serving those whom the Lord has sent." I was looking at what people were doing and missing what God was doing. As a people pleaser, I was taking my signals from the wrong source.

I learned that I am not in this pastoral profession to please people; I am in it to please God. The question is not how many leave, not even how many join, but from whom you are taking the signals. Stop trying to please people, and look at what God has done. Twenty-five years later we've got 2,500 at each worship service three times each Sunday! We've got more folks in the choir than we had in the entire congregation back then! The content, what God is trying to say to you, might be far more important than the specifics of your supplication. God is drawing you closer to Himself.

Elijah was a people pleaser, like me. He was taking his signal from people, from the wrong source. Look at 1 Kings 19:2-3. When Jezebel sent Elijah a threat, "Boy am I going to get you," Elijah took his signals from Jezebel instead of from the one who had made Jezebel. Verse 3 says Elijah was afraid. People pleasers will always be afraid. Elijah was afraid for his life. He was taking his signals from the wrong source, and God in the content of his response had to straighten things out for Elijah.

God said, "Come here. Be still and know." The wind came by to split mountains, but it didn't blow Elijah one bit. An earthquake destroyed from Sinai to Damascus, but the preacher was unharmed. God said, "Just be still and know I give the orders here, Elijah. Not Jezebel. I want you to know who I am." Then there was the fire reminiscent of Carmel, and Elijah wanted to run back into the cave. God said, "You're forgetting something, Elijah. Just be still and know that I am God. You get your signals from me. Don't take your signals from Jezebel."

Sometimes our seemingly unanswered prayer is God's way of telling us, "I heard what you've been asking for, but I want you to want *me* more than you want *things*. Just be still and know." In the stillness of the practice of prayer, there is another great thing to be learned. So many times we think of getting out of difficulty into the comfort of prayer. That's why Karl Marx called religion an opiate, an escape from reality. But Marx was wrong. Authentic prayer is not an escape hatch, an opiate, getting out of the fight via flight into illusion, no, no, no. Authentic prayer is what gives us the courage to stay in the battle. Prayer is not a retreat from danger; prayer is the secret source of courage to go back out there and face whatever comes.

Look at the content of God's answer to Elijah in verses 15-18. The Lord said, "Return. Go back where you came from. I am with you. And I have seven thousand more who have not bowed. Go on back. Don't give up. Get up!" Stay in constant communion with the one who is the I Am to every need. Even when it seems as if your prayers are not being answered, keep on praying. It is in prayer that we put our roots down deep into the limitless reservoir of God's strength, not our strength! When we tell God we are tempted to give up as Elijah did, that it's too much, when we tell God we are dangerously close to being swallowed up or drowned by our problems, then the Lord gives us the stamina to be steadfast and unmovable. Just stay in that constant communion with God, and see if you don't hear him tell you as he told Elijah, "Don't give up; I'm with you. Don't give up; keep pressing on toward the mark of the high calling. Don't give up; this race is in your grasp. Don't give up; I didn't bring you this far just to leave you! Don't give up; there is no limit to the perseverance I'll give you if you just give me the glory. Don't give up. Weeping may endure for a night, but don't give up, because joy is coming in the morning. Don't give up! I didn't give up my Son for nothing. Don't give up. I'm just as near to you down in this valley as I was on the mountain. Don't give up."

Appendix

*Goals of and Outline for Organizing a Local Church Prayer Ministry**

"The effectual fervent prayer of a righteous man
availeth much." —James 5:16

Goals:

To develop cohesiveness within the membership.

To develop a spirit of fellowship in the entire membership.

To encourage prayer throughout the entire membership.

To encourage members to become more conscious of God
and prayer.

To improve prayer life of individuals.

To strengthen members as individuals through prayer.

To strengthen the membership through prayer.

To develop a unified fellowship of disciples—

who are full of the Holy Spirit;

who possess joy, peace, and love;

who continually love mercy, do justly, and walk humbly
with God;

who, being of one accord, exercise the privilege to come
boldly to the throne of grace, to obtain mercy, and to
find help in time of need;

who recognize their authority in Christ Jesus;
who will wage war against enemies of the soul;
who pray for children, youth, adults;
who pray for the healing of social ills;
who pray for the needs of the membership and the
    ministries of the church,
who pray for the witness of Christ in the world.

Outline

I. Discuss and designate responsibilities of prayer team.
    A. Develop plans for continuous emphasis on prayer in
       the church.
    B. Teach praying.
       1. To new members class
       2. To leaders of prayer workshop
II. Form a prayer team.
    A. Choose members who hunger and thirst for God.
    B. Choose members who are serious students of Scripture.
    C. Choose members who are committed to the discipline
       of prayer.
III. Develop an annual workshop on prayer (Matthew
     18:19; James 5:16).
    A. Invite entire membership to attend.
    B. Require attendance of church leaders.
IV. Emphasize prayer for new members (Hosea 4:6).
    A. Provide new members with material on prayer.
    B. Staff membership room with a member of the prayer
       team.
V. Emphasize prayer in the new members class.
    A. Provide comprehensive material on prayer as vital to
       Christian living.
    B. Introduce scriptural passages dealing with prayer (for
       example, Deuteronomy 9:18; 2 Chronicles 16:11;
       7:14; Isaiah 58:9; Hosea 4:6; Matthew
       18:19; 26:41; Acts 4:24; Philippians 1:3-4; 1 Timothy
       2:1-2; Hebrews 4:16; 12:1; James 5:16).

    C. Introduce different kinds of prayer:
       1. Adoration
       2. Praise
       3. Petition
       4. Intercession
       5. Consecration
       6. Dedication
       7. Communion
    D. Provide a refresher course on prayer every six months.
VI. Provide prayer partners for church members.
VII. Establish a prayer month.
    A. Emphasize prayer for an entire month each year.
    B. Have appropriate staff and prayer team members at the church twenty-four hours a day.
    C. Be sure telephones are covered and doors are open.
    D. Offer all-night prayer on certain days.
    E. Publicize prayer month using posters, flyers, and banners.
VIII. Establish a weekly prayer night (Luke 6:12).
    A. Designate a regular day and time, such as each Sunday at 6:00 P.M.
IX. Organize prayer cell groups (Matthew 18:19).
    A. Divide entire membership into groups on the basis of where they live.
    B. Select a leader or team leaders for each group.
    C. Select a biblically inspired name for each cell group.
    D. Have each group select a day or night each month for meeting together in fellowship and prayer.
    E. Have each cell group develop a prayer chain.
       1. Activate prayer chain in the event of needs or emergencies.
X.   Establish all-church prayer hour.
    A. Designate a particular hour of each day as a prayer hour.
    B. Urge members to enter into prayer at the designated time.

XI. Designate vehicle, such as a prayer box, for facilitating
     prayer requests.
   A. Place prayer-request box in the church.
   B. Direct prayer team to collect and pray over requests two
      times during week.
XII. Develop a prayer support team.
   A. Discuss and designate responsibilities of a team to
      volunteer Spirit-filled, dedicated prayers to provide
      prayer coverage for pastor and pastoral staff.
   B. Direct team to pray over various assignments.
   C. Direct team to pray over travel itineraries.
   D. Direct team to provide continuous prayer coverage
      for those in leadership.
XIII.Designate vehicle, such as prayer wheels, for
     facilitating weekly prayer emphasis.
   A. Determine the subject of each wheel, such as church,
      family life, social issues, city, and nation.
   B. Create various poster-sized prayer wheels.
   C. Designate and announce from pulpit specific prayer
      emphasis each week.
   D. Duplicate the wheel and include in Sunday's bulletin
      as a reminder of the members' need to pray daily.

---

* Prepared by Cheryl Elliott, minister in training and prayer coordinator of Allen Temple Baptist Church.

DATE DUE